I0840591

RIO-MAR-APR/2000 - Letters on March - Page 5 - Nr. 280

Gilberto Freyre: one century

Teacher ANTÔNIO LOULÉ

On March 15, 1900, when finishing the called CENTURY OF THE LIGHTS, he was born in SANTO ANTÔNIO OF APIPUCOS, PERNAMBUCO, that that would be, according to the universal consensus, the most brilliant of the Brazilians, the man that would illuminate the character, the formation, the culture, the race, the physical and moral morphology of the "homo brasiliensis".

Brazil owes GILBERTO FREIRE a lot (to Portugal also), and we waited that in the year of his centennial our compatriots from Portugal want to render to his memory the homages that it deserves. As for us, Portuguese from Brazil, we have more than obligation, we have interest in proclaiming our admiration for the that is very exactly considered as the most powerful born intelligence to the south of Ecuador. Actually, the prodigious intellectual from Pernambuco was an ardent defender of the Portuguese colonization, and the "poor politics" that tends to minimize him as sociologist just gets to disrespect itself own.

His larger work, BIG HOUSE & SLAVE QUARTER, that defends with immense wisdom and no smaller heat the miscegenation (besides constituting the best picture of Brazil that was already become pregnant), it was published in 1933, year in that Hitler ascended to the power in Germany and, with him, the ideas and practices racists that would end for taking to the Holocaust. On that time, the Fascist ideas collection had wide audience in GETÚLIO VARGAS'S BRAZIL (him even a Dictator of Right, to the time), and it lacked little (or it didn't lack anything) so that SIR GILBERTO FREYRE (the title was attributed him by the Queen of England) a dangerous left radical was considered. Today his defense of the Portuguese colonization does with that sections of the same left of Brazil and of Portugal they make to put to forget and to be forgotten his monumental work, which, if it is impossible in the countries of English language and in the remaining educated countries (excepted Japan, where only now will be translated), it is going being unhappily a fact in the ingrate countries of Portuguese language. We waited that, at least in Brazil, the Centennial of the master's birth annuls the current horizon view, that can be defined by the following circumstance: when commercial shows of mass as the movies, the quick music and even rock festival reaches releases protection (and budgets) of the Ministry and of the State General offices of Culture, the posthumous work of the founder of the BRAZILIAN SOCIOLOGY deteriorates in trunks sealed in Pernambuco.

Plus: a meticulous work of compilation, of revision of the translations and of rising of the origin of each text, done by EDSON NERY DA FONSECA, teacher retired "emérito" of the University of Brasília and entitled according to own Freyre, REPATRIATED WORDS AND ANTICIPATIONS, it still didn't get patronage to be edited, what represents a couple loss to Brazil, for the called countries of Portuguese official language and to for the universal literature. Because GILBERTO FREYRE, besides an educated and innovative sociologist and historian, is also a writer of first water.

Only a great writer, for instance, would be capable of the conciseness ironic and at the same time exact of this paragraph, with that he opens a chapter on our MAFRA in the book ADVENTURE AND ROUTINE:" I review MAFRA. Grandiose but banal the old convent. A Portuguese Spaniard without Spanish's genius for the Spaniards." And after this apparent redundancy, only increases still with singular synthesis spirit: " (...) this Portuguese monument, less expression of authentic greatness than of magnificence an amount simulated..." Who sits down for MAFRA an indefinable sensation of work of forgers of the religion, art, of the architecture and to of the greatness - and they are many the Portuguese that seat it, it cannot leave so far, his fact to get right in full in the (maybe) only Portuguese monument that transmits this strange sensation.

Of rest, the whole vision of Portugal that GILBERTO FREYRE adopts as his daughter and the one that gives verbal expression, it is fruit of a love and admiration almost without limits.

Index

Page66

SHOULDER TO SHOULDER. April 2000. Page 11. Nr. 143.

NATIONAL SHAME

Lieutenant-colonel Osmar José of Barros Ribeiro

Recently, the newspapers announced that the planted area is decreasing year to year in Brazil and that will spend more than 1 billion and half of dollars in the import of victuals. We should matter, to example of previous years, rice of Thailand, bean of Mexico, wheat and corn of Argentina, making the happiness of the importers and the despair of the Government money authorities.

Brazil has vast extensions of arable lands and, second estimate of the National Confederation of the Agriculture, same taking into account our low productivity, fruit of the scarce available technology in the field, they could almost be picked three hundred million tons of grains, case was explored the area conveniently still available, guaranteeing the internal provisioning and the existence of surpluses for export. They miss the agriculture, in general lines, a politics of minimum prices, net of silos for stockpiling, cheap credit, safe to do face to the climatic unexpected, etc., it is worth to say, an Agricultural Politics.

While this and other problems are minimized and played for the days which will never come, the news section taken to the great public's knowledge speaks of disputes around the increase of the parliamentarians' salaries and of the members of the Judiciary Power, turning shameful the news as for the increase of the minimum wage. Of the re-establishment of the salary levels of those members of the Executive Power, except of the ones that they possess advantage with exclusion of somebody else and against the right common holders of " positions of superior advice", they speak nothing, as if the cost of living was felt only by parliamentarians, judges, promoters, " and crowd ".

Really, as say one of the national television commentators, " that is a shame".

Index

Page67

Shoulder to Shoulder. April 1999. Page 10. Nr. 131

He alerts the youths!

Colonel Carlos Alberto Brilhante Ustra

My book, " Breaking the Silence ", published in 1987, about my performance in the Military detachment of Operations of Information (DOI), II Military Brazilian Region, (September 29, 1970 to January 1974), it was dedicated to the youths, because most of the allured for the subversion and the terrorism was constituted of youths explored for old and communist militant experts. Those young ones were manipulated and used as " cannon " scouring pad while their people who convinced them made their heads and they played them in front of combat in an useless violence, taking them to assault, to kill and to kidnap. The old communist leaders, always in the rearguard, they used as argument to justify the terrorism actions the fact of they be struggling " to free Brazil of the military dictatorship."

Today, twelve years later, again I write thinking about the youths that ignore that part of the history, in the youth soldier, sergeant, lieutenant, captain, in the labor youth, doctor, lawyer, journalist, teacher - finally in the youth reformer, idealist, pure of spirit and of intentions and that again is being used. They continue making them the head, making other think as they think. Improvised historians, journalists with the old leaders' same ideologies, full of retaliation, write distorted versions, introducing guerrilla fighters and terrorists as innocent students that they went " massacred " by torturers to service of the dictatorship ".

In the reality, the Revolution of 31 of March of 1964 was a reaction to the totalitarian ones that, infiltrated in president João Goulart's government, they intended to establish a "República Sindicalista", without consent of the National Congress, counting with the masses worker's rebellion and student.

There are several decades the Soviet Union tried to implant the communism in Latin America, having had success in Cuba. In 1968, starting from Carlos Marighella's ideas, that he thought about the force of the weapons, if it intensified the attempt of the rural and urban guerrilla's implantation in Brazil. For this several terrorist organizations, all Marxist-Leninist ones were created. Their members, preferably young students and workers, were correspondents to communist countries, mainly Cuba, where they received instructions on the handling of light and heavy weapons, explosives, guerrilla tactics, communications, First Aid, survival in the jungle, conduct in urban and rural operations.

When they returned, those young ones enter for the secrecy, they abandoned their families, their studies, their jobs, changed their names through false documents and they became terrorist and professional guerrilla fighters.

The terrorist organizations, for to they maintain in action, they needed a lot of money. In spite of they receive the foreigner's many resources, they started to assault banks and cars payers and they began to terrify the country with violent actions: attempted the bomb, assaults to barracks, murders, ambassadors' kidnapping, kidnapping of airplanes, assaults to vehicles policemen and sentries of barracks. They began, also, the agitation in the student and labor way, unchaining political strikes, protest marches, riot and widespread frolic.

While the terrorists established the insecurity in the main cities of the country, other groups began rural guerrilla in the area of Araguaia. The guerrilla fighters objective was to implant a liberated area where the Brazilian government could not enter, as it happens today in Colombia, in a larger area than the one of Switzerland.

They intended the rural guerrilla fighters, leaving of the field, to reach the cities, that they would be dominated already by the urban terrorists, for then, uniting forces, to drop the government and to create a communist republic in the molds of the Cuban dictatorship.

The police was impotent to combat them. With the policemen's losses - died and wounded - it became more and more reared.

As the situation of the country was day by day more serious, to try to reestablish the order the Institutional Action it was decreed Nr. 5. Even so, as they continued if intensifying the terror actions, a Presidential Guideline was sent. According to her, the Military Commanders of Area became the responsible for the Safety Interns in their areas of responsibility, besides for the combat to the terrorism and the subversion. To advise them, they were created, also for the Presidential Guideline, Council of Defense Intern (CONDI), the Centers of Operations of Defense Intern (CODI). As operational force of CODI was formed Military detachment of Operations of Information (DOI).

The Centers of Information of the Navy (CENIMAR), of the Aeronautics (CISA) and of the Army (CIE) they also participated of the process.

They DOI were them subordinated the bosses of the Second Sections of the Military Commands. Besides the commanding major of the DOI, the Army participated of their crew with some captains and sergeants. Most of the personnel was originating from of the police civilian and state military police. In São Paulo, our crew belonged to 250 men.

It was in that situation of internal war that those organs, today so criticized, they began to act centralizing the information and the combat actions. Like this, we entered in that fight that we didn't begin, didn't want and that, in any hypothesis we could lose her, under penalty of our terms subdued Homeland the a left totalitarianism.

Our enemy was violent and it killed with coldness. He was an enemy constituted by ideological professionals and prepared tactics manners that acted among the population, they attacked of surprise and they were extremely cruel in action. In his majority they were not " innocent " students but yes guerrilla fighters well.

In 1964, we went winner when we impeded that " under physical forces " a Republic Syndicalist of Marxist-Leninist stamp was implanted.

You that didn't live the called years of lead, see in this small summary the escalade of the terror that devastated the country and that the media forgets to remind:

· (DD/MM/YY) 25/07/66 - Airport of Guararapes, Recife. A bomb explodes with the objective of killing the President. Killed journalists Edson Régis Carvalho and admiral Nelson Gomes Fernandes. Wounded the, today, general Sylvio Ferreira of Silva and more 13 people, besides a 6 year-old child.

· 25/01/68 - The traitor and deserter Carlos Lamarca steals of the 4th. Regiment of Infantry 63 rifle FAL, 5 machine guns INA and a lot of ammunition.

· 26/06/68 - A kombi full of explosives is played against the General Barracks of II Exército/São Paulo. The explosion lacerated soldier's Mário Kozel Filho body and it hurt 3 soldiers.

· 22/07/68 - Assaulting to the Military Hospital of São Paulo and robbery of rifles FAL.

· 12/10/68 - THE captain of the North American army Charles Chandler, that took a course in Brazil, it is murdered in front of his wife and their children in the door of his house in São Paulo.

· 04/09/69 - THE American ambassador Elbrick is kidnapped.

· 11/03/70 - Kidnapping of the General consul of Japan Nobuo Okuchi in São Paulo.

· 10/05/70 - Carlos Lamarca and his group kill to his blows prisoner lieutenant Alberto Mendes Júnior that he had surrendered to him so that yours commanded, wounded in confrontation with the group of Lamarca, they could receive medical service. His body was only found 4 months later.

· 11/06/70 - Kidnapping of the ambassador of Germany, Von Holleben. Terrorists kill Moura Régis's agent Irlando, they hurt agent Luís Antônio Sampaio seriously and slightly Silva's agent José Banharo that they made the ambassador's security.

· 27/10/70 - Sergeant of the Aeronautics Valder Xavier Lima with died with a shot in the nape for the terrorist Theodomiro Romeiro of Santos that prisoner was driven in a military vehicle.

· 07/12/70 - Kidnapping of the Swiss ambassador Giovanni Eurico Bucher.

· 03/04/71 - Major José Júlio Toja Martinez, dead when making the prison of a couple of terrorists of MR8.

· 15/04/71 - Henning Albert Boilesen, industrial murdered by terrorists in the city of São Paulo.

· 05/02/72 - David Cuthberg, 19 years, sailor of an English frigate is killed in Rio de Janeiro by " belonging to an imperialistic nation."

· 25/02/73 - Otávio Gonçalves Moreira Júnior, police chief, belonged to DOI/II Army. Shot at the beach of Copacabana where, in vacations, it took a shower at sea.

To the whole, we had 105 died and 343 wounded, some of the which became disable.

To purpose, the magazine VEJA, of 27/05/98. It informed that the current Boss of Armed Force General Staff would have declared regarding the military actions of combat to the terror: the military action in that period was not institutional. Some military people participated, no the armed forces. It was a parallel action."

Actually, our action was institutional, because the organ to which we belonged had been created by a Guideline of the President and all of us were designated officially for DOI. Besides we were subordinated to the Military Commanding generals of Area, from who we received orders and we continued subjects to the same laws, regulations, promotions and it disciplines soldierly of the other companions of the Army.

It is right that the crew of the ones that acted in the combat to the terrorism was small. But to affirm that for we be 1% of the cash of the Army didn't represent the armed forces, it is the same as to say that the Brazilian Army was not present in São Domingos, Suez or Angola because the crew there employed was not superior to the of a battalion.

Yes, we were very few, but, the mission was accomplished and our work was recognized . Many of us received the medal of the Pacifier with Palm, the highest condecoration of the Brazilian Army, granted to those that executed the duty life risk. Us, the combatants of the DOI, not only we took a risk our lives, but, also, the one of our families. Some died and others were wounded, and we are the aware of the accomplished duty. Those few struggled so that the peacefulness returned to the Country and so that the remaining of the armed forces worked with peace in the barracks again, in the schools and in the cabinets.

We expired many battles and we lost others.

In 1964, we went winner when we impeded that in the " arbitrary mood " a Republic Syndicalist of Marxist-Leninist stamp was implanted.

Another victory was terms ended with the terrorism, what did with competence. In that war, the number of deads, on both sides, was not superior to 500, while in the neighboring countries the losses were very larger.

Colombia, that until today fight against the terrorism, already lost more than 30.000 lives.

Unhappily we lost a very significant battle: the one of mass communication. The due ones distort the facts and they deceive the people, mainly the youth. They want, through the lie, to write the history with their version and they are going getting their objective. There is a certain cowardice in counting the truth to the new generations. Happily the hard-working and peaceful citizen that they lived those times don't need of that because they felt the threat of the terrorism and they were not upset by the repression.

As very well it mentioned it writter Olavo of Carvalho, it was " the military Government's own softness that it allowed the enthronement of the leftist lie as official history. Disabled for any armed action, the left took refuge in the universities, in the newspapers and in the movement editorial, installing her main trench " there (O GLOBO, 19/01/99).

Undeniably we won the war against the Marxist dictatorship. And when that period, in the future, it comes to be written with exemption and without passions, our work will be recognized and the armed forces, particularly the Brazilian Army, they will be presented as the great barrier that impeded that Brazil became a communist satellite. The elimination of the terrorism allowed that it returned the full democracy that today we enjoyed, we always wanted and that we deserved, because it is of our nature, civil and military.

Next

Page68

Shoulder to Shoulder. April 99. Page 11.

That you are warned against the fury of the legions

Colonel Paulo Fernando Hecht da Fonte
From the appearance of our human species, never equality existed among the human beings. As we are social animals there was always who ordered and who obeyed in the groups.

It is curious to observe that the today said military were the first ones to pour. The audacity, the force, the ability in the handling of the weapons and the necessary courage to use them did with that them if they imposed wants as hunters, he/she wants as warriors, maintaining the survival. The first tribe bosses, of clan, were " military men ", it may be said this... Political men, being faced the Politics with letter P capital letter there, as the art of creating the development of the nations and the good to be of the people, they took them the stick of the command, although of them they always needed at times bitterness.

To the military it was infused that he/she should stay far away from the politics, to be always the " moral " reservation. I remember of being so innocent that the great appeal that made to announce me of the Revolution of March 31, 1964 was the break of the hierarchy! This yes, it was of my understanding. We are not entitled more today of staying in way so alienated.

The right is that today, in all of States, an official said group exists, that it leads it in way political-administrative, economical and sacred. It is made calculations that the Official Group is constituted of 5% of the population. This, it goes itself, it is not good nor bad, it is a statistical verification. It is also statistical that exist in every State unhappy that create a group Anti-official, that it is opposed to the that are in the power, mainly for ideas, ideals and ideology. About 15% of a people it belongs to that group. The others 80% are among the Rocking ones, some times supporting one, other times another of the groups in confrontation.

The mental processes of the dominant group, always "monadistas" and "maximocrata", base on the said central brain (cerebellum and trunk), linked to the survival, maintenance, to power, wealth, politics and administration. The one of the group Anti-official use of the brain left, rational, logical, scientific researcher and analyst. The great Rocking group has the prevalence of the brain right, affectionate, creative, "holístico", spiritualized...

All of them can have a performance positive or negative. When the group that is in the power is positive, he seeks, although "maximocrata", to distribute the wealth and too much satisfactory among the whole population (not for kindness, but for wisdom!). Search the roll-neck golden, or that is the balance point where 62% of the population have access to 38% of the goods! If this happened there would be " general Happiness of the Nation!"

In Brazil, however, 10% of the population detains 90% of the goods - it is a breakdown, an unsustainable ignominy! The neo-liberalism has a Charles Darwin´s vision - the most capable will survive. Only that the great master of the evolution of the species had a biological focus, no cruel as the socioeconomic focus of our days.

What does make our group Anti-official, done act priorly by Party of the Workers (PT) and their followers of the Movement Without Land (MST)? They maintain the same vision dialectics, didacticism and outdated of the Marxism-Leninism, swept of almost everyone, but no swept of the minds full of useless revenge of certain political ones Brazilian.

Definitively we should not count to the inequality cruel neo-liberal, not to the Marxist Utopian equality and yes to the possible and desirable proportional way!

And the one what do us, the guarantors of the regime? Yes, because same " dressing pajamas " I refuse to give up my patent.

In a book of Jean of Larteguy on warriors in Indochina and in Algeria, the following words exist:

" They had in the statement, when we left the birthplace, that we left in defense of the sacred rights that they are checked to us by so many citizens installed there far away, so many years of presence, so many benefits granted to the populations that have need of our aid and of our civilization.

We could verify as that was true, and, because it was true, we didn't hesitate in spilling the tax of the blood, in sacrificing our youth, our hopes. We didn't lament anything, but while here this state of mind encourages us, they say that in Rome the intrigues and the conspiracies are happened, the betrayal is developed and that many, hesitant, disturbed, they give in with easiness to the worst temptations of the abandonment and them abase our nation.

I beg you, it tranquilizes me you the more possible abbreviation and you tell me that our fellow citizens understand us, they defend us, they protect us like us own we protected the great Empire. If all this was different, if we had to leave our bones abandoned whitened on the tracks of the desert, then, be careful against the fury of the Legions! Marcus Flavínius - Centurion the 1st. Cohort of the August Legion, for his cousin, Tertulius, in Rome ".

Next
May 2000, page 5, from "Shoulder to Shoulder", e-mail ombro@ombro.com.br

Title: Joio e o trigo.

Author: Mrs. Rogéria Bolsonaro, member of legislative house of city Rio de Janeiro.

Mais uma vez chega ao nosso conhecimento através da mídia um escândalo envolvendo políticos. Para não nos afastarmos muito no tempo, iniciemos pelos "anões do orçamento"; "Collorgate"; "Precatórios" e agora o "Pitagate".

Em todos estes escândalos o que parece coincidência, tornou-se rotina. Vejamos a sequência:

1º, aparece a denúncia;

2º, desacreditam o denunciante chamando-o de louco, desequilibrado ou outro motivo;

3º, colocam o denunciante na justiça, invertendo-se o fato, o acusado passa a acusador;

4º, lentidão da justiça e procrastinação;

5º, PIZZA mass for everybody.

Assim aconteceu com o denunciante do escândalo do orçamento que está preso por outro motivo, mas os envolvidos verdadeiramente estão impunes; aconteceu com Pedro Collor que escapou de alguma punição porque morreu; neste escândalo a única peculiaridade foi a saída de Fernando Collor de Melo do poder mais por forças políticas do que pelo crime em si, pois os demais envolvidos, passando pelas outras fases, acabaram na massa de pizza; os precatórios tiveram o mesmo caminho.

Estamos vivendo o clímax do escândalo político de São Paulo.

A senhora Nicéa Pitta ainda está na primeira fase, isto é, denunciando, porém já foi considerada insana desequilibrada, logo estará na condição de acusada, possivelmente tenhamos um "bode expiatório" e também terminará na 5ª fase: PIZZA.

É de se lamentar que somente os insanos e desequilibrados sejam honestos. É de se lamentar que tenhamos poucos insanos nos meios políticos, para que outros escândalos venham à tona.

No clamor destes acontecimentos, eu concito os eleitores a refletirem além da indignação. Este é o momento de separar o "joio" do "trigo". É a oportunidade de separar os bons políticos daqueles sem escrúpulos - os maus políticos.

O seu julgamento é mais rápido do que a própria justiça, o prazo máximo dura somente quatro anos.

Prezado eleitor, toda vez que você tiver esta oportunidade de julgar o bom e o mau, não deixe passar, não seja conivente com mais uma pizza (meaning people involved for and against a subject will have a heavy plate of pizza for all of them; it will not be solved.)

Go back

May 2000, page 5, from " Shoulder to Shoulder ", e-mail ombro@ombro.with.br

Title: Joio and the wheat.

Author: Mrs. Rogéria Bolsonaro, member of legislative house of city Rio de Janeiro.

Once again it arrives to our knowledge through the media a scandal involving political. For us not to move away ourselves a lot in the time, let us begin for the " dwarfs of the budget "; Collorgate "; Precatórios " (communes´debts originated from law decisions against them) and now " Pittagate ".
In all these scandals that it seems coincidence, it became routine. Let us see the sequence:

1st, he/she appears the accusation;

2nd, they discredit the accuser calling him lunatic, unbalanced or other cause;

3rd, they put the accuser in the justice, being inverted the fact, the accused raisin to accuser;

4th, slowness of the justice and procrastination;

5th, PIZZA mass goes everybody.

It happened like this with the accuser of the scandal of the budget that is arrested for other cause, but involved them are truly unpunished; it happened with Pedro Collor that escaped from some punishment because he died; in this scandal the only peculiarity was the exit of Fernando Collor de Melo of the more power for political strengths than for the crime in itself, because the others involved, going by the other phases, they ended in the pizza mass; the "precatórios" had the same road.

We are living the climax of the political scandal in São Paulo.

Nicéa Pitta is still in the first phase, that is, denouncing, however it was already considered insane unbalanced, soon it will be in accused's condition, possibly have a " scapegoat " and it will also finish in the 5th phase: PIZZA.

It is of lamenting that only the insane and unbalanced are honest. It is of lamenting that we have few insane ones in the political means, for other scandals to come to the surface.

In the clamor of these events, I incite the voters to reflect it besides the indignation. This is the moment of separating the " joio " of the " wheat ". It is the opportunity to separate the good politicians of those unscrupulous one - the political bad.

His/her trial is faster than the own justice, the maximum duration lasts only four years.

Dear voter, every time that you have this opportunity to judge the good and the bad, don't
let to pass, be not conniving with one more pizza (meaning people involved goes and
against the subject will have the heavy plate of pizza goes all of them; it will not be solved.)

Go back

Negritude e Poder

Autor: Pedro Carneiro

Negritude e Poder

Caxias-MA, 1985

Direitos Autorais Reservados

Reserved copyrights

NOTA SOBRE O AUTOR

ANTONIO PEDRO CARNEIRO é piauiense de Teresina. Suas atividades profissionais levaram-
no a residir em Caxias-MA, cidade que lhe concedeu o título de Cidadão Honorário e onde
tem permanecido por mais de trinta anos. Além de professor, tem exercido cargos públicos
na administração estadual e municipal.

DEDICATÓRIA
Ofereço este livro aos homens de todas as raças que, em qualquer parte do mundo, lutaram
e sacrificaram suas vidas, na luta contra os fanatismos, os preconceitos e as injustiças
sociais.

O Autor

ÍNDICE

Author: Pedro Carneiro

Blackness and Power

Caxias, Maranhão, Brasil, 1985.

Reserved copyrights

Reserved copyrights

NOTE ON THE AUTHOR

ANTONIO PEDRO CARNEIRO is State of Piaui´s born in the city Teresina. His professional activities took him to live in Caxias-MA, city that granted him Honorary Citizen's title and where he has been staying for more than thirty years. Besides teacher, he has been exercising public positions in the state and municipal administration.

DEDICATION

I offer this book to the men of all of the races that, in any part of the world, they struggled and they sacrificed their lives, in the fight against the fanaticisms, the prejudices and the social injustices.

The Author

INDEX

INTRODUÇÃO

Este livro é, antes de tudo, uma pequena contribuição para o despertar do homem negro, no Brasil. É, também, um roteiro e uma mensagem, especialmente para os jovens negros, de modo a encararem de frente e com determinação a realidade de hoje como uma preparação para a realidade de amanhã. Não deixa de ser, também, o extravasar da revolta e da indignação que toma conta de todas as mulheres e homens negros, contra a prática cotidiana do racismo, cada vez mais crescente, no Brasil, chegando a constituir-se em ameaça aos direitos constitucionais dos cidadãos negros, sem que, qualquer manifestação de repúdio à prática da discriminação racial, seja observada por parte do Estado ou das instituições que se dizem democráticas.

Ao que parece, a discriminação racial contra o negro tem tido, até aqui, o apoio tácito dos órgãos de comunicação, notadamente a televisão, e do Governo, este, pela omissão, e aqueles, pelas reportagens parciais em que deixa subjacente o preconceito contra o homem de pele negra.

INTRODUCTION

This book is, before anything, a small contribution for the black man's awakening, in Brazil.
It is, also, an itinerary and a message, especially for the black youths, in way they face it in
front of them with determination the reality today as a preparation for the reality tomorrow.
It doesn't stop being, also, extravasating of the revolt and of the indignation that takes
control of all of the women and black men, against the daily practice of the racism, more
and more growing, in Brazil, getting to constitute in threat to the black citizens'
constitutional rights, without, any rejection manifestation to the practice of the racial
discrimination, be observed on the part of the State or of the institutions that are said
democratic.

To that seems, the racial discrimination against the black has been growing, here, with the
tacit support of the communication organs, especially the television, and of the
Government, this, for the omission, and those, for the partial reports in that they leave
underlying the prejudice against the man of black skin.

Na verdade, a deflagração de um movimento pacífico, mas vigoroso, como forma de
protesto e de repúdio à discriminação racial existente no país, é tarefa intransferível dos
próprios negros. eles, e somente eles, devem ser os protagonistas desta batalha, contra as
forças que os oprimem.

QUEM FOMOS, QUEM SOMOS E O QUE SEREMOS

A verdade sobre o negro brasileiro contada por um negro.

Humilhações e vexames a que estão submetidos as mulheres e homens negros, no Brasil.

In the truth, the explosion of a movement peaceful, but vigorous, as protest form and of
rejection to the existent racial discrimination in the country, it is untransferable task of the
own blacks. To them, and only them, they should be the main actors of this battle, against
the forces that oppress them.

WHO WE WERE, WHO WE ARE AND WHO WE WILL BE

The truth on the Brazilian black counted by a black.

Humiliations and shames the one that the women and black men are submitted, in Brazil.

QUEM FOMOS NÓS

Não importa, se viemos do Oeste ou do Sudoeste do continente africano; se chegamos aqui, no Brasil, no século XVI ou XVII; se vivíamos como príncipes ou como plebeus; se pertencíamos a uma tribo paupérrima ou poderosa e rica. O que importa considerar é que éramos livres, na miséria ou na riqueza; o que sobreleva e conta é que fomos, de fato, sequestrados pelo homem branco europeu, seja ele inglês, holandês ou português, acorrentados e presos nos porões dos navios, levando chicotadas e sofrendo toda sorte de privações e sofrimentos inenarráveis.

WHO WE WERE

It doesn't matter, if we came from the West or of the Southwest of the African continent; if we arrived here, in Brazil, in the century XVI or XVII; if we lived as princes or as plebeians; if we belonged to a tribe very poor or powerful and rich. The one that imports consider is that we were free, in the poverty or in the wealth; the one that bolds and bill is that we were, in fact, kidnapped by the European white man, be him English, Dutch or Portuguese, chained and arrested at the basements of the ships, taking whippings and suffering every luck of privations and sufferings words cannot describe.

E, aqui, chegamos. Como escravos, submetidos a trabalhos de toda ordem e sem nada receber em troca, a não ser castigos e punições e ofensas morais de toda ordem; um tipo de escravidão diferente daquela a que eram submetidos, desde a Idade Antiga, os que perdiam sua liberdade na derrota nos combates; uma escravidão humilhante que não nos permitia ao menos conviver com nossos irmãos de tribo, privando-nos do prazer de dialogar e conversar com nossos irmãos de tribo, privando-nos do prazer de dialogar e conversar em nosso próprio dialeto; e trabalhamos e sofremos; com nosso trabalho e com nosso suor construímos a grandeza deste país; a cana-de-açúcar e o seu ciclo usou e abusou da força dos nossos braços e de nossas mãos calosas para o incremento dessa agricultura; enriquecemos a terra tornando-a produtiva e, muito mais ainda, enriquecemos o senhor-de-engenho que a nós nos tinha como escravos e como seus animais de tração. Tudo isso aconteceu em pleno Cristianismo e sob o olhar complacente e, porque não dizer, cúmplice do Clero que, às vezes, chegava a tirar vantagens pecuniárias à custa do tráfico negreiro e da consequente escravidão dos negros; e, pior ainda: Tem-se o descaramento de falar-se em Abolição da Escravatura, nos compêndios históricos oficiais, como se isso, de fato, tenha acontecido, como um ato de magnanimidade e compaixão da monarquia que detinha o poder em 1888.

Abolição com flores - reza a História - em contraposição a que se fizera, nos Estados Unidos, com sangue. E que ganhamos com essa falsa abolição? O abandono, o desamparo, o "olho da rua"; um modo muito humano e cômodo do patrão ficar livre dos escravos que durante muitos anos o servira, como um cão fiel ao seu dono; e o que recebemos em retribuição, quando não pelos olhos da justiça e pelos ditames da lei - que nunca existiu para os pretos - ao menos pela lei moral que se grava na consciência de todo homem de bem? Nada, absolutamente nada. Nem um pedaço de chão que todo escravo que trabalhara a terra do senhor, anos a fio, teria direito, para que nela pudesse trabalhar e manter decentemente sua família. Não mais precisavam de nós; o banguê cedia lugar à usina; chegava-se à indústria; queria-se gente melhor preparada para a nova era que surgia; negro não servia, pois era analfabeto; analfabetismo que os próprios senhores-de-engenho e os demais senhores de escravos sempre tiveram o maior empenho em manter os escravos, tratados como animais e que só serviam para o trabalho braçal. Aprender a ler e a escrever, apenas os brancos tinham esse direito. Por que não os imigrantes europeus? Os negros que fossem para o quinto dos infernos; o que podiam dar em trabalho já lhes havia sido tirado. Que fossem viver debaixo das árvores, sem ter alimentação, vestuário ou qualquer outra necessidade própria aos seres chamados humanos; negro não era ser humano; nascera apenas para servir, servir, servir, sem nada reclamar.

And, here, we arrived. As slaves, submitted to works of every order and without anything to receive in change, just to receive punishments and punishments and moral offenses of every order; a slavery type different from that the one that was submitted, from the Old Age, the ones that lost their freedom in the defeat in the combats; a humiliating slavery that it didn't allow us at least to live together with our tribe siblings, depriving us of the pleasure of to dialogue and to talk with our tribe siblings, depriving us of the pleasure of to dialogue and to talk in our own dialect; and we worked and we suffered; with our work and with our perspiration we built the greatness of this country; the sugarcane and its cycle used and it abused the force of our arms and of our callous hands for the increment of that agriculture; we enriched the earth turning her productive and, much stiller, we enriched the gentleman-of-mill that had us as slaves to us and as their traction animals. All this happened in the middle of the Christianity and under the compliant glance and, because not to say, accomplice of the Clergy that, sometimes, it got to remove financial advantages at the expense of the traffic slave trader and of the consequent slavery of the blacks; and, worse still:

The shamelessness is had of speaking in Abolition of the Slavery, in the summaries historical officials books, as if that, in fact, have happened, as an action of magnanimity and compassion of the monarchy that it stopped the power in 1888. Abolition with flowers - it says the History - in opposition the one that had been made, in the United States, with blood. And that did we win with that false abolition? The abandonment, the abandonment, the "eye of the street"; a very human and comfortable way of the boss to be free from the slaves that it had served him for many years, as a dog faithful to his owner; and the one what received in retribution, when not for the eyes of the justice and for the dictates of the law - what did never exist for the blacks - at least for the moral law that is recorded in every man's conscience of well? Nothing, absolutely nothing. Nor a ground piece that all slave that had worked the earth of you, for years, would have right, so that in her he could work and to maintain his family honestly. No more they needed us; the "banguê" gave up place to the plant; it was arrived to the industry; prepared better people were wanted for the new era that was appeared; black didn't serve, therefore it was illiterate; illiteracy that the own gentleman-of-mill and the other gentlemen of slaves always had the largest pledge in maintaining the slaves, treaties as animals and that they were only for the manual work. To learn to read and to write, just the whites were entitled. Why no tthe European immigrants? The blacks that went to the fifth of the hells; what could give in work had already been them removed. That they will live under the trees, without having feeding, clothing or any other own need to the called humans; black was not human being; he had just been born to serve, to serve, to serve, without anything to complain.

Não era homem, como os demais homens; era filho do diabo e não de Deus, Pai de todos, como o Cristo havia ensinado.

E esta concepção e este tratamento desumano e ignóbil tem continuados até os dias de hoje e tem sido a base sobre a qual se tem erguido todo o processo discriminatório que se assiste diariamente neste país e nesta chamada "democracia multiracial", que, na prática, como regime, beneficia apenas alguns e deixa na marginalização a totalidade da população que não tem acesso ao consumo dos bens e nem participação na distribuição da renda nacional.

He was not man, as the other men; he was the devil's son and not of God, Father of all, like Christ had taught.

And this conception and this inhuman and ignoble treatment has been continuing until the days today and it has been the base on which it has been raising the whole discriminatory process that it is attended daily at this country and in this call "multiracial democracy" , that, in practice, as regime, it benefits just some and it leaves in the marginalization the totality of the population that doesn't have access to the consumption of the goods and nor participation in the distribution of the national income.

O QUE SOMOS HOJE, NA SOCIEDADE BRASILEIRA

Não há a menor sombra de dúvida que, nós os pretos, hoje somos, na sociedade brasileira, os mesmos escravos que fomos no Brasil-colônia e no Brasil-império. O tipo de habitação de que os negros dispõem, não é o mesmo; é pior, apesar de ter mudado o nome. Não se chama mais senzala; é favela; não é mocambo; é palafita. Os bancos de praça ou as calçadas ou debaixo de pontes são habitações por demais conhecidas e utilizadas por nós, nas grandes cidades. Nossos filhos, com raríssimas exceções, sofrem toda sorte de discriminações, na escola e nos demais lugares onde se agrupam crianças brancas, asiáticas e negras; aqueles que conseguem, a todo custo, conquistar um título universitário, sofem mais ainda, por entenderem e sentirem quando estão sendo discriminados, às vezes de modo solerte, insidioso e covarde, não aberta, mas veladamente. Veja-se, como exemplo, o caso do Esporte, no Brasil. No basquete e no vôlei, masculino ou feminino, apenas um ou dois atletas de cor negra figuram nos times respectivos; são todos por demais conhecidos: Édson, no masculino de basquete; Marta ou Janete, no basquete feminino; no vôlei a cousa não é diferente; enquanto em Barcelona o fantástico Dream-team americano apresentava apenas um jogador branco em sua equipe de basquetebol masculino, a nossa representação nesta modalidade era inteiramente o inverso; no vôlei, apenas um jogador negro. E não é o bastante: Há, ainda, para tais jogadores o chamado tratamento aumentativo-pejorativo muito a gosto de certos locutores e comentaristas de TV. Não se chama Marta; é "martona"; não é Ronaldo (futebol); é "ronaldão"; tais epítetos são pronunciados com o único objetivo de mostrar a presumida superioridade racial ou para estigmatizar, para evidenciar que esse ou aquele atleta é negro. Portanto, na cabeça de quem os pronuncia, ser negro é ser diferente dos demais homens ou dos demais seres humanos; há, também, a discriminação para os juízes de futebol: Se o árbitro é negro, não é bom árbitro, não presta; sobre ele caem todas as críticas maldosas e, às vezes, até cusparadas na cara, como aconteceu em São Paulo, quando um árbitro de cor negra teve sua cara cuspida por um canalha que se diz civilizado e jogador de futebol. Pode ser um péssimo árbitro, parcial e ladrão, mas se for branco, tudo nele é minimizado por nossa hipócrita máquina de comunicação falada e escrita. Esse insidioso e desumano tratamento com que são "aquinhoados" tem contribuído e até mesmo estimulado o surgimento de alguns grupos de desajustados, com idéias próprias ou importadas, como o recente surgimento de grupos chamados neonazistas, que, na verdade, nada mais são que uma reprodução mal engendrada de grupos racistas como a Klux-Klux-Klan americana. Poderíamos, ainda, falar de alguns programas de televisão onde, via de regra, são mostrados ao público e ali mesmo "indiciados sem julgamento, quase tão somente os infratores de cor negra e, quando o infrator é um branco, o delito cometido é minimizado, o tratamento chega a ser benevolente, por quem faz a reportagem. Na verdade, o que se procura mostrar a essa hipócrita sociedade, é que os criminosos são apenas os negros e que estes devem ser vistos como criaturas nocivas ao convívio social e, portanto, indignas de qualquer atenção por parte dos poderes constituídos e da sociedade brasileira. E ainda há muito mais. Se você é preto ou mulato ou pardo-escuro, em resumo, se você é preto e possui instrução média ou superior, observe o que se passa em seu redor, por causa de sua presença, quando você toma um transporte coletivo qualquer, trem, ônibus ou lotação. Se você toma um assento que está vago, a pessoa a seu lado, branca, evidentemente, pelo gesto com que lhe vira o rosto, pela maneira como procura segurar firmemente a bolsa ou outro objeto que conduza, faz com que você passe a repudiar tais pessoas, e, por uma questão de brio e de vergonha na cara, você passa a viajar em pé, tomando solavancos, mas, ao menos sem sentir golpes morais, em decorrência da cor de sua pele. Você, branco ou branca, que lê estas linhas, já imaginou se isso acontecesse com você ou com seus filhos ao tomar um transporte coletivo? Certamente você se sentiria magoado, ferido em sua dignidade, não de homem branco, mais de pessoa humana, como ocorre também com as criaturas humanas de cor preta, que a toda hora são brutalmente massacradas e vilipendiadas em seus direitos e em sua estrutura moral e espiritual de pessoas humanas, da mesma gênese que as demais criaturas que habitam o Planeta Terra.

WHAT WE ARE TODAY, IN THE BRAZILIAN SOCIETY

No there is to smallest doubt shadow that, us the blacks, today we are, in the Brazilian society, the same slaves that we went in the Brazil-colony and in the Brazil-empire. The house type that the blacks dispose, it is not the same; it is worse, in spite of having changed the name. He doesn't call himself more slave quarter; it is slum; it is not "mocambo"; it is stilt. The square banks or the sidewalks or under bridges they are houses for too much known and used by us, in the great cities. Our children, with rare exceptions, suffer every luck of discriminations, in the school and other places where group White children, Asians and Black; those that get, at all costs, to conquer an academical title, suffer deeper, for they understand and they feel when they are being discriminated, sometimes in covered way, insidious and cowardly, no open, but shadowsly. See it, as example, the case of the Sport, in Brazil. In the basketball and in the volleyball, masculine or feminine, just one or two athletes of black color represent in the respective teams; they are all for too much known: Édson, in the masculine of basketball; Marta or Janete, in the feminine basketball; in the volleyball the matter is not different; while in Barcelona fantastic American Dream-team just introduced a white player in it team of masculine basketball, our representation in this modality was entirely the inverse; in the volleyball, just a black player. And it is not enough: There is, still, for such players the call augmentative-pejorative treatment a lot appreciated by certain announcers and commentators of TV. He doesn't call himself Marta; it is "martona" (big marta); he is not Ronaldo (soccer); it is "ronaldão" (big ronaldo); such epithets are pronounced with the only objective of showing the conceited racial superiority or to stigmatize, to evidence that or that athlete is black. Therefore, in the head of who pronounces them, to be black is to be different from the other men or of the other human beings; there is, also, the discrimination for the soccer judges: If the referee is black, he is not good referee, it doesn't render; on him all the wicked critics fall and, sometimes, even to blow mouth liquid´s on the face, as it happened in São Paulo, when a referee of black color had his face spit by a rabble that is said civilized and soccer player. He can be a terrible referee, partial and thief, but if it goes white, everything in him is minimized by our hypocrite machine of spoken communication and writing. That insidious and inhuman treatment with that they are "target to receive as a valued gift" has been contributing and even having stimulated the appearance of some groups minded messed up, with own ideas or brought from abroad, as the recent appearance of groups called neo-Nazi, that, in truth, they are not more than a badly engendered reproduction of racists groups as American Klux-Klux-Klan. We were able to, still, to speak of some television programs where, as it is a rule, they are shown to the public and there even "accused without judgement", almost so only the offenders of black color and, when the offender is a white, the committed crime is minimized, the treatment gets to be benevolent, for who makes the report. In truth, what she tries to show to that hypocrite society, it is that the criminals are just the black color and that these should be seen as noxious creatures to the social conviviality and, therefore, unworthy of any attention on the part of the constituted powers and of the Brazilian society. It is there still much more. If you are either mulatto or brown-darkness black, in short words, if you are black and it possesses instruction medium or superior, observe what happens in the circuit around you, because of your presence, when you take any public transportation, train, bus or small rented cars for many people (vans). If you have a seat that is vague, the person to your side, white, evidently, for the gesture with that she turns away from you the face, for the way as she tries to hold the bag or other object that she carries, firmly, it makes that you start to reject such people, and, for a subject of pride and of shame in the face, you start to travel in foot, taking jolt, but, at least without feeling moral blows, due to the color of your skin. You, white man or white woman, who reads these lines, did you already imagine that happened with you or with your children when taking a public transportation? Certainly you would feel hurt, wounded in your dignity, not of white man, but of human person, as it also happens with the human creatures of black color, that at all times are massacred brutally and reviled in their rights and in their moral and spiritual structure of human people, of the same genesis that the other creatures that inhabit the Planet Earth.

A SITUAÇÃO ECONÔMICA DOS NEGROS, NA ATUAL SOCIEDADE BRASILEIRA

Como no passado, até aqui o lema tem sido: Trabalhar muito e receber pouco ou nada; como não têm acesso às fontes do saber, salvo pequenas exceções, aos pretos brasileiros outra opção não lhes resta senão o trabalho braçal, como aliás vêm fazendo ao longo desses quase cinco séculos da vida nacional. Daí o poder aquisitivo do homem ou da mulher negra ser quase reduzido a zero. Como a renda familiar não dá nem para alimentação dos que compõem a família, inevitável se torna a falta de habitação e a total incapacidade de prover os filhos do necessário para que tenham uma vida digna e decente como pessoa humana. Como não têm acesso à escola de nível médio, pois geralmente não conseguem concluir o curso fundamental, por motivos óbvios, dificilmente podem os negros chegar à universidade. Quando não é "menino de rua", dado o estado de pobreza total da família, a partir dos sete anos já começa a trabalhar fazendo pequenos serviços de modo a poder contribuir com algum dinheiro para ajudar no orçamento doméstico da família.

A ECONOMICAL SITUATION OF NEGROES, IN THE CURRENT BRAZILIAN SOCIETY

As in the past, here the slogan has been: To work a lot and to receive little or nothing; as they don't have access to the sources of knowledge, except for few exceptions, to the Brazilian blacks other option doesn't remain them except the hand work, as in fact they are making those along almost five centuries of the national life. Then the black's purchasing power or of the black woman to be almost reduced to zero. As the family income doesn't give nor for feeding of the ones that compose the family, inevitable if it turns the house lack and to total incapacity of providing the children of the necessary that they have a worthy and decent life as human person. As they don't have access to the school of medium level (high school), because they don't usually get to conclude the fundamental course, for obvious reasons, difficultly they can the blacks to arrive to the university. When he is not "street boy", given the state of total poverty of the family, starting from the seven years he already begins to work doing small paid services to contribute with some money to help in the domestic budget of the family.

Nessa fase, ou a partir dessa fase, pode a escola do crime e da marginalidade ganhar mais um sócio, um aluno; é a fase mais vulnerável para o menino ou para o adolescente ser aliciado pelos marginais e entrar, de fato, na marginalidade, ingresso quase sempre de difícil retorno. Isso ocorre, como ficou dito, em decorrência de falhas estruturais de natureza política e social, relativamente ao descaso que o país vem dando ao negro a partir de sua chegada ao Brasil até aos nossos dias e, mais significativamente, a partir de 1888, ano da suposta "libertação".

In that phase, or starting from that phase, it can the school of the crime and of the delinquency to win one more partner, a crime student; it is the most vulnerable phase for the boy or for the adolescent to be allured by the marginal ones and to enter, in fact, in the delinquency, entrance almost always of difficult return. That happens, as it was said, due to structural flaws of political and social nature, relatively to the disregard that the country is giving to the black starting from his arrival to Brazil to our days and, more significantly, starting from 1888, year of the supposed "liberation."

O crime maior que o Estado brasileiro cometeu, ou se quiserem, a Monarquia, foi o de não preparar o negro para que pudesse viver fora das senzalas, pois os que detinham o poder e os meios de produção não tiveram a visão voltada senão para seus interesses econômicos e políticos, relegando os escravos à condição de abandono, penúria e miséria.

The largest crime that the Brazilian State committed, or if they want, the Monarchy, was it of not preparing the black so that he could live out of the slave quarters, because the ones that holded the power and the production means didn't have the vision focused except for their economical and political interests, relegating the slaves to the condition of abandonment, poverty and misery.

Competiria à Monarquia usar de seu poder, nos poucos dias que lhe restavam, para assentar as bases sobre as quais a Primeira República pudesse consolidar algumas medidas imperiosas, no campo econômico e no campo político, para que os negros pudessem trabalhar e produzir e construir um pequeno patrimônio que lhes possibilitasse participar dignamente, com seus filhos, da vida nacional. Não seria pedir muito; o longo período de escravidão trabalhando a terra, quando não pelo ponto de vista jurídico - pois eram escravos - mas pelo senso natural das coisas e pelo direito incrustado na consciência de todo homem de bem, lhes daria direito a uma gleba dessa mesma terra para o cultivo de cereais, de modo a alimentar a família e comercializar o excedente, diminuindo substancialmente o número de miseráveis, por um lado, e, por outro, enriquecendo o patrimônio nacional.

It would compete to the Monarchy to use of its power, in the few days that it would remain there before loosing Power, to seat the bases on which the First Republic could consolidate some urging actions , in the economical field and in the political field, so that the blacks could work and to produce and to build a small patrimony to make possible to do business with it exceeds, that it would permit him and his children to participate with dignity of the national life. It would not be to ask a lot; the long slavery period working the earth, when not for the juridical point of view - because they were slave - but for the natural sense of the things and for the right incrusted in every man of good path's conscience, he would give right to a field of that same earth for the cultivation of cereals, in way he feeds the family and to market the surplus, reducing substancially the number of miserable, on one side, and, for other, enriching the national patrimony.

Tivesse isso sido feito e não teríamos hoje o inchaço populacional nas grandes cidades brasileira; ter-se-ia evitado o êxodo rural; a criminalidade teria hoje taxas bem menores que as apresentadas estatisticamente; é quase certo que não teríamos os chamados "meninos de rua" ou pequenos marginais a assaltar e roubar os indefesos habitantes das cidades.

It had that been done and we would not have the population growing without control today in the great Brazilian cities; it would have avoided the rural exodus; the criminality would have much smaller taxes today than presented statisticaly; it is almost for sure that would not have the called "street boys" or little bandits to assault and to steal the defenseless cities inhabitants.

Aí estão as causas mais significativas que originaram o quadro de criminalidade que se observa hoje no Brasil. E o que faz o poder público? Fecha os olhos a tudo isso; segue a política do "laissez-faire", do "deixa estar para ver como é que fica"; ou, como se supõe, não pode conciliar interesses populares com interesses de poderosos; a terra não é para o povo; é para alguns latifundiários que a tem cercada de arame farpado ao longo desses anos todos, desde a distribuição das sesmarias no século XVI. É uma posse duvidosa;

There they are the most significant causes they originated the criminality picture that is observed today in Brazil. And what does the one make the public power? It closes the eyes to all this; it follows the politics of the "laissez-faire", of the "let it be to see how it will be"; or, as it is supposed, it cannot reconcile popular interests with powerful people interests; the earth is not for the poor people; it is for some landowners that it has been surrounding it with barbed wire along these whole years, from the distribution of the "sesmarias" (lands given by the King to his nobles) in the century XVI. It is a doubtful ownership;

Enquanto isso, o povo pobre, os pretos, pardos e mulatos deste país continuam esperando que alguma coisa seja feita, em nome da justiça, justiça esta que até os céus continuam a clamar que um dia seja realizada, para que, os menos favorecidos da fortuna, os carentes de tudo e de todos, os "descamisados", possam ter um dia a satisfação de se sentirem pessoas operantes, integradas na sociedade e participantes do progresso e da riqueza nacional.

Enquanto esse dia não chega, o que se pode dizer é que, no momento, é de penúria e miséria, a situação econômica dos negros, no Brasil.

Meanwhile, the poor people, the blacks, brown and mulattos of this country continue waiting that some thing is made, on behalf of the justice, justice this that it continues to shout until the skies that one day is accomplished, so that, those least favored of the fortune, the lacking ones of everything and of all, the undressed shirts ("descamisados"), can have one day the satisfaction of feeling effective people, integrated in the society and participants of the progress and of the national wealth.

While that day doesn't arrive, what it can be said is that, in the moment, it is of poverty and misery, the economical situation of the blacks, in Brazil.

A SITUAÇÃO POLÍTICA DOS NEGROS, NO BRASIL

Por viver em uma chamada "democracia multiracial", seria de pressupor-se que os negros, politicamente, vivessem num mar de rosas, pois a democracia, pelo menos em tese, é o governo do povo. Sendo a nossa uma democracia representativa - como geralmente a rotulamos - o Congresso deve, necessariamente, representar o povo, elaborando leis que consultem aos interesses e aspirações populares, fiscalizando os atos do Poder Executivo, além de outras atribuições que lhe são conferidas na Constituição Federal.

A POLITICAL SITUATION DOS NEGROS, IN BRAZIL

For living in a call "democracy multiracial", it would be of presupposing that the blacks, politically, lived in a sea of roses, because the democracy, at least in theory, it is the government of the people. Being our a representative democracy - as we usually labeled it - the Congress must, necessarily, to represent the people, elaborating laws to consult to the nterests and popular aspirations, supervising the actions of the Executive Power, besides other attributions that are granted it in the Federal Constitution.

Quando usamos a expressão "governo do povo e "democracia representativa", devemos atentar para o fato de que, na prática, a coisa é diferente. Primeiramente, vejamos a situação cultural do povo que está sob essa democracia. De um lado estão os que não estão na escola e aqueles que, embora tenham sido matriculados, não concluíram, por razões diversas, o curso fundamental; aqueles, analfabetos e, estes, semi-analfabetos, sem autonomia de leitura; do outro lado encontram-se poucos que estão no segundo grau e, pouquíssimos, os que chegam à universidade.

When we used the expression "government of the people and "representative democracy", we should look at the fact that, in practice, the thing is different. Firstly, let us see the cultural situation of the people that is under that democracy. On a side they are the ones that are not at the school and those that, although they have been enrolled, they didn't end, for several reasons, the fundamental course; those, illiterates and, these, semi-literate persons, without reading autonomy; on the other side they are few that are in the second degree and, very few, the ones that arrive to the university.

Em termos comparativos, para que se tenha uma idéia aproximada da educação brasileira, hoje, relativamente ao que foi apresentado no último censo demográfico, em 1980, extraímos alguns tópicos do livro "Educação, Economia e Estado, de Martin Carnoy, 3ª Edição, 1984, onde se lê no prefácio de Ladislau Dowbor, páginas 5 a 7, o seguinte:

In comparative terms, for an approximate idea of the Brazilian education to be had, today, relatively to the that was presented in the last demographic census, in 1980, we extracted some topics of the book "Education, Economy and State, of Martin Carnoy, 3rd Edition, 1984, where it is read in Ladislau Dowbor's foreword, pages 5 to 7, the following:

"Brasil 1982: São 125 milhões de habitantes, dos quais cerca de 27 milhões nas escolas. Destes, 23 milhões estão no primeiro grau, somente 2,9 milhões no segundo grau e 1,3 milhões de privilegiados que chegam ao ensino superior"... e mais adiante:

"Brazil 1982: They are 125 million inhabitants, of the which about 27 million in the schools. Of these, 23 million are in the first degree, only 2,9 million in the second degree and 1,3 million privileged that they arrive to the higher education"... and further on:

Para já, em termos quantitativos, somos um país de 32 milhões de analfabetos. (PNAD, 1982, IBGE), ou seja, praticamente um terço da população em idade de ler e escrever. Isto num mundo onde as necessidades de conhecimentos crescem rapidamente. Se acrescentarmos a população que tem entre um e quatro anos de estudo - e, num país sem infra-estruturas de cultura popular, uma pessoa que se limitou a quatro anos de estudo raramente cria autonomia de leitura e capacidade de auto-instrução - chegamos a um total de 61 milhões de pessoas, frente aos 91 milhões de pessoas de mais de dez anos de idade.

For already, in quantitative terms, we are a country of 32 million illiterates. (PNAD, 1982, IBGE), in other words, practically a third of the population in age of reading and writing. This in a world where the needs of knowledge grow quickly. If we increase the population that has between one and four years of study - and, in a country without infrastructures of popular culture, a person that was limited to four years of study rarely creates reading autonomy and self-instruction capacity - we arrived to a total of 61 million people, front to the 91 million people of more than ten years of age.

Em outros termos, dois terços da nossa população não tem estudo nenhum, ou no máximo até o quarto ano. A situação que enfrentamos, neste plano, apresenta-se simplesmente como de marginalização educacional do grosso da população. Esta marginalização decorre evidentemente de problemas estruturais mais amplos.

In other terms, two thirds of our population don't have study any, or in the maximum until the fourth year. The situation that we faced, in this glides, it simply comes as of educational marginalization of the thick of the population. This marginalization elapses evidently of wider structural problems.

No relatório do Banco Mundial de 1982, o Brasil aparece como único país onde os 10 % mais ricos das famílias consomem mais da metade do produto social. (The World Bank-Brasil, Washington, 1982)". Compare-se esses dados com a situação atual e veremos que a coisa não mudou muito. E o "grosso da população" a qual se refere o autor é constituído, indubitavelmente, de pretos e mulatos. Para reforçar o que afirmamos, leia-se, ainda, este tópico:

In the report of the World Bank of 1982, Brazil appears as only country where the richer of the families 10% consume more of the half of the social product. (The World Bank-Brasil, Washington, 1982)." It is compared those data with the current situation and we will see that the thing didn't change a lot. And the "thick of the population" which refers the author is constituted, undoubtedly, of blacks and mulattos. To reinforce what affirmed, be read, still, this topic:

"Em 1982, 61 % das pessoas ocupadas ganhavam dois salários-mínimos ou menos, situando-se claramente na faixa da pobreza. Mas esta situação trágica em termos econômicos atinge 69 % das mulheres, 70,1 % dos mulatos, 77,5 % dos negros... Para mulheres negras, a cifra atinge 84 %. Para o homem branco, 48,7 %. (PNAD, 1982 - IBGE, Brasil e Grandes Regiões, página 27)."

"In 1982, 61% of the busy people won two wage-minima or less, locating clearly in the strip of the poverty. But this tragic situation in economical terms reaches 69% of the women, 70,1% of the mulattos, 77,5% of the blacks... For black women, the figure reaches 84%. For the white man, 48,7%. (PNAD, 1982 - IBGE, Brazil and Great Areas, page 27)."

Face ao exposto, é fácil concluir-se que o povo brasileiro, em sua grande maioria, não é politizado; e não o é porque essa grande maioria é constituída de homens e mulheres desprovidos de cultura, incapazes portanto, de saber o que são seus direitos e seus deveres políticos e sociais. Quanto à democracia representativa", cabe a seguinte indagação: Representativa de quem? Você responderá que ela é representativa do povo; mas, de que povo, se a maioria desse povo, apesar de votar e ser votada, é constituída de analfabetos ou de semi-alfabetizados, portanto, incapaz de votar e eleger conscientemente os seus representantes? Logo, não têm representatividade; os eleitos pelo voto são representantes não desse povo mas daqueles que detêm o poder econômico e que pressionam os congressistas para que votem as leis que são do interesse de suas empresas, de suas associações, e que vetem aquelas que venham a contrariar esses mesmos interesses.

Face to the exposed, it is easy to end that the Brazilian people, in its great majority, it is not politicized; and it is not it because that great majority is constituted of men and women without culture, unable therefore, of knowing that are their rights and their political and social duties. As for the "representative democracy", the following inquiry fits: Representative of who? You will answer that it is representative of the people; but, what people, if most of this people, in spite of voting for and to be voted for, is it constituted of illiterates or semi-literate, therefore, unable to vote for and to choose their representatives consciously? Therefore, they don't have representativeness; the elect ones for the vote are representatives not of that people but of those that hold the economical power and that they press the members of Congress so that they vote for the laws that are of the interest of their companies, of their associations, and that they veto those to come to contradict those same interests.

A grande maioria vota mas não participa do processo democrático; geralmente o voto é dado em troca de algum benefício material ou mesmo vendido para algum poderoso que pretenda eleger um parente ou alguém que venha a representar seus interesses ou de sua empresa. esses e tão somente esses têm representantes no legislativo.

The great majority votes for but it doesn't participate in the democratic process; usually the vote is given in exchange for some material benefit or even sold for some powerful one that he intends to choose a relative or somebody that comes to represent their interests or of his company. those and only those have representatives in the legislative.

Conquanto se reconheça que a Constituição Brasileira assegura a todos o livre exercício da cidadania e, consequentemente, o pleno gozo dos direitos civis e políticos, na prática, os negros continuam alijados (excluídos) do processo e da representação política, dado os motivos e fatores já analisados, o que mostra que a situação política dos homens e das mulheres negros, no Brasil, ainda é de marginalização.

Although it is recognized that the Brazilian Constitution assures all the free exercise of the citizenship and, consequently, the full joy of the civil laws and political, in practice, the blacks continue smuggled (excluded) of the process and of the political representation, given the reasons and factors analyzed already, what shows that the men's political situation and of the women blacks, in Brazil, it is still of marginalization.

OS NEGROS E A PENA DE MORTE

A pena de morte, se instituída no Brasil, por certo iria se constituir numa verdadeira espada de Dâmocles a pairar sobre a cabeça dos negros brasileiros e daqueles outros que não dispusessem de recursos financeiros para litigar nos processos criminais em que figurassem como indiciados.

Não pretendemos entrar no mérito das razões de ordem moral, filosófica ou teológicas, que possam justificar, ou não, a implantação da pena de morte no Brasil.

Apenas diremos que, tirar a vida de alguém, qualquer que seja a maneira ou os meios utilizados, constitui crime, não apenas sob o ponto de vista jurídico, mas também sob as concepções teológicas, éticas, filosóficas e morais. Implantando a pena de morte, o Estado estaria, também, legalizando o assassínio, ocupando, portanto, o mesmo lugar dos criminosos.

THE BLACKS AND THE DEATH PENALTY

The death penalty, if instituted in Brazil, for sure it would constitute in a true sword of Dâmocles to hover on the head of the Brazilian blacks and of those others that didn't have financial resources to fight in the criminal processes in that they represented as accused.

We didn't intend to enter in the merit of moral order reasons, philosophical or theological, that they can justify, or no, the implantation of the death penalty in Brazil.

We will just say that, to remove the life of somebody, any that is the way or the used means, it constitutes crime, not just under the juridical point of view, but also under the theological, ethics, philosophical and moral conceptions. Implanting the death penalty, the State would be, also, legalizing the murder, occupying, therefore, the criminals' same place.

E, quem seriam os condenados? Nem é preciso pensar para responder, se considerarmos que apenas os pobres estão nas cadeias públicas e que a justiça, via de regra, protege os que dispõem de influência política ou de poder econômico-financeiro, enfim, que dispõem de recursos para litigar junto aos tribunais, teríamos, de resto, apenas os deserdados da fortuna, os carentes, os pobres; noutras palavras, os pretos é que iriam compor a fila dos sentenciados à morte pelo Estado, e, muitas vezes, injustamente condenados.

Por outro lado, não deixaria de ser uma maneira fácil de se eliminar um grupo social; seria um novo holocausto, como os nazistas fizeram com os judeus ao longo da segunda Guerra Mundial.

And, who would the convicts be? Nor it is necessary to think to answer, if we consider that just the poors are in the public chains and that the justice, as a rule, protects the ones that dispose of political influence or holders of economical-financial power, finally, that they have resources to fight in tribunals close to, we would have, of rest, just disinherited them of the fortune, the lacking ones, the poors; in other words, the blacks are that would compose the line of the sentenced to the death by the State, and, a lot of times, wrongly convicts.

On the other hand, it would not stop being an easy way to eliminate a social group; it would be a new holocaust, as the Nazi did with the Jews along to Second World War.

O QUE FAZER PARA MUDAR O QUADRO ATUAL

Todas as realizações humanas, quaisquer que sejam os campos de atividade, trazem imanente uma força propulsora que faz transformar sonhos e idéias em realidade concreta.

Diríamos que essa força, esse elemento responsável pela dinamização dos meios necessários à consecução de um objetivo, chama-se PODER. Talvez aí esteja o motivo pelo qual, ao longo da história e até aos nossos dias, o negro americano tenha lutado e se organizado, para conseguir o respeito que hoje tem em seu país.

Para comprovar o que afirmamos, poderíamos citar, como exemplo, apenas alguns cargos de relevo que são atualmente (1995) ocupados por indivíduos negros, nos Estados Unidos da América:Governador de Estado, Presidente da Suprema Corte de Justiça, Chefe do Estado-Maior das Forças Armadas.

WHAT TO DO TO CHANGE THE CURRENT PICTURE

All of the human accomplishments, any that are the activity fields, bring immanent a leading force that makes to transform dreams and ideas in concrete reality.

We would say that that force, that responsible element for the dynamization of the necessary ways to the attainment of an objective, it is called POWER. Maybe there it is the reason for which, along the history and to our days, the American black has struggled and organized himself, to get the respect that today has at his country.

To prove what affirmed, we could mention, as example, just some relief positions that are now (1995) fulfilled by black individuals, in the United States of America: Governador of State, President of Supreme court, Chief of Armed Forces Joint-commanders-staff.

No Brasil, salvo raríssimas exceções (como no Governo atual, ex-jogador de futebol (Pelé, Ministro Extraordinário dos Esportes e um ou dois parlamentares no Congresso Nacional) procuramos distinguir algum indivíduo negro desempenhando um alto cargo público e não encontramos nenhum. Os pretos não têm representação política, o que implica dizer que também não dispõem de poder político, chave através da qual se abririam as portas para que alguns representantes da raça negra pudessem participar da administração e da vida política do país.

O modo como os negros se encontram, nesse imenso espaço para formar a base sobre a qual se assentará, um dia, a pirâmide do poder político, econômico e social, é quase impossível se pensar em termos de representação, como possuem os negros americanos. Aliás, já é por demais sabido, a representação política é uma projeção da força advinda das associações organizadas política e juridicamente. Esses propósitos encontrarão sempre, no caminho de sua realização, forças antagônicas, sendo uma delas a discriminação racial.

Segundo o pensamento de alguns entendidos, a discriminação racial constitui um disfarce para assegurar a continuidade do poder político e da dominação econômica. Quanto às associações, embora existam no país algumas entidades que congregam homens e mulheres de cor negra, o que se pode dizer é que elas apenas procuram apresentar ao público atividades esportivas, recreativas e folclóricas, objetivando, ao que parece, tornar conhecida a cultura negra ou afro-brasileira. É como se trocassem a forma pelo conteúdo, o acessório pelo principal; tais manifestações não levam a nada, podendo, às vezes, até ter um sentido negativo, na medida em que servem de críticas e de juízos pejorativos por parte daqueles que vêem, no negro, tudo de ruim.

In Brazil, except for rare exceptions (as in the current Government, soccer former-player (Pelé, Extraordinary Minister of the Sports and one or two parliamentary in the National Congress) we tried to distinguish some black individual carrying out a high public position and we didn't find anyone. The blacks don't have political representation, it implicates to say that they don't also have political power, key through which they would open up the doors so that some representatives of the black race could participate in the administration and of the political life of the country.

The way as the blacks remain, in that immense space to form the base on which will settle, one day, the pyramid of the political, economical and social power, is almost impossible to think in representation terms, as they American blacks possess. In fact, it is already for too much known, the political representation is a projection of the force that comes from the associations, organized politics and juridically. Those purposes will always find, in the road of their accomplishment, antagonistic forces, belonging one to them the racial discrimination.

According to the thought of some experts, the racial discrimination constitutes a disguise to assure the continuity of the political power and of the economical dominance. As for the associations, although they exist at the country some entities that congregate men and women of black color, what can be said it is that they just try to present to the public sporting, recreational and folkloric activities, aiming at, as that seems, to turn the culture black or Afro-Brazilian known. It is as they changed the form for the content, the accessory for the main; such manifestations don't lead to anywhere, being able to, sometimes, even having a negative sense, in the mood that they serve as critics and of pejorative judgements from the part of those that see, in the black, everything of bad.

Para que o negro brasileiro possa sair da situação marginal e caudatária em que se encontra, torna-se necessário a obtenção do poder, através da união de todos, num bloco uno, coeso, congregando pretos, pardos e mulatos, para agirem como um conjunto organizado política e juridicamente; que as organizações existentes se agrupem em torno de uma entidade diretora, em âmbito nacional, para, por meio dela, reivindicarem seus direitos; que, nos pleitos eleitorais, elejam seus próprios candidatos, aqueles que tenham compromissos com a libertação dos negros, com a reversão e mudança do quadro atual; que pugnem, enfim, para que o negro tenha uma vida decente e digna e que seja respeitado pelos demais segmentos da sociedade brasileira.

Separados, continuaremos a ser esmagados, como o temos sido até agora; unidos, haveremos de vencer; união é força, é poder. E, sem este poder, nada conseguiremos; o PODER somos nós. E, com ele, poderemos nos libertar dos grilhões que nos prendem à miséria e à marginalização social, econômica e política; com ele adquiriremos os meios necessários que haverão de nos conduzir a uma vida decente e digna, sem subserviência, sem humilhações; nossos filhos passarão a ser olhados como criaturas humanas, que são, e não como sub-raça, como seres inferiores; poderemos, então, encarar a todos com sobranceria, em condições de igualdade, como pessoas e como cidadãos iguais que somos; poderemos prescindir daqueles que se dizem racialmente superiores; não mais andaremos nos rebaixando servilmente, para conseguir um emprego, uma ocupação, na competição com o homem branco. Tudo isso fará com que nos sintamos orgulhosos de nós mesmos e com a consciência tranquila de havermos cumprido a nossa missão, ao lançar os alicerces de uma nova estrutura social, política e econômica, em benefício dos negros, no Brasil.

So that the Brazilian black can leave the marginal situation and tailed position that he is, it becomes necessary obtaining the power, through the union of all, in a single block, united, congregating blacks, brown and mulatto, for us to act as a organized politics and juridically group; that the existent organizations group around a managing entity, in national ambit, for, through it, to demand our rights; that, in the elections, choose our own candidates to have commitments with the liberation of the blacks; with the reversion and change of the current picture; that they fight, finally, for the black to have a decent and worthy life and that it is respected by the other segments of the Brazilian society.

Separated, we will continue to be squeezed, as we have been it up to now; united, we must win; union is force, it is power. And, without this power, nothing we will get; the POWER is us. And, with it, we can free ourselves from the metal chains that arrest us to the poverty and the social economical and politics marginalization; with it we will acquire the necessary means that they must lead to a decent and worthy life, without subservience, without humiliations; our children will become looked as human creatures, that they are, and not as a sub-race, as inferior beings; we will be able to, then, to face all with eyes to eyes, in conditions of equality, as people and as same citizens that we are; we can abstract of those that racially superior say to themselves; no more we will have been being lowered serverly, to get a job, an occupation, in the competition with the white man. All this will do with that we feel proud of us ourselves and with the calm conscience of we have accomplished our mission, when throwing the foundations of a new social, politics and economical structure, in benefit of the blacks, in Brazil.

Composed and printed paper in the Leaf of Caxias´ Graphics.

Shoulder to Shoulder. May 2000. Page 6.

Partners, ALERT!

General Hélio Ibiapina Lima *

With this title, the Magazine of the Military Club, in the month of February 2000 published his EDITORIAL with the objective of alerting the partners, in matter to the that still meet in the active service, for the dangers that patrol us around the system "previdenciário".

Carefully we showed that there were a lot of promises, nothing else than promises, repeated since 1994, that the military ones would have a system own "previdenciário".

When in 1997/98 we were considered, for Law, just military, differentiated of the other servants of the Union, everything took to have faith that they would be accomplished them reiterated promises of a substantial increase and a peculiar precaution.

He had, then, more active pursuit, the action interministerial, under coordination of Brazilian Armed Force General Staff (EMFA), to elaborate the bill "Previdenciária" and New Law of Remuneration of the Military ones.

Elaborated a Project of Law for the Military, after having analyzed for the Military Ministers, it was introduced to the President with a very argued Exhibition of Reasons.

The Comission Interclubs constituted by 9 partners that advise the three Presidents of the Military Clubs, it elaborated a sketch of Project of Precaution, with base in Fund to be managed by the own associates, entirely independent of National Treasury and that it would usually be applied to market interests. Copies were sent Senators and Deputies.

EMFA, as it informed, not even it considered our suggestion for a system of peculiar precaution to the military ones.

Meanwhile the Government tried to collect contribution of the retired ones (unconstitutional decision). The retired ones moved unconstitutionality action and the Superior Federal Tribunal (STF) it defeated the Government's intentions for 11 x 0.

The decision of STF irritated the Government that decided to present to the Congress deeply, the Project of Constitutional Amendment (PEC) that took the number 136, that it proposes new contribution level for the civil servants and constitutionalize the collection of the retired ones.

In a secret manner, harnessed the Precaution of the Military ones to PEC in walking, forgetting all about the promises since 1994/95.

That decision, that affects the military ones deeply, above all the one of the active, it constitutes a manifestation of unrestricted hate, to the armed forces, that we cannot recognize as legitimate manifestation and, much less, aided in any concept of justice.

Later, the President determined that MD kept the bill presented by the Military Ministers until that the problem of the collection of the retired ones was solved, then it would retake the problem so that the military ones returned to the initial position: framing in the General System of Precaution.

ABEMIFA, for inspiration of Col. José Aldo Peixoto Corrêa published the Editorial in esteem, in his informative nº. 63 of abril/2000, with prominence.

Besides the following note was put: " In time: Many companions are strange to the gravity of the moment and they think that they are entitled, when the truth is not that. Before the facts, it would be interesting that all of the associations of military existent in the Garrisons, congregating officials, sublieutenants and sergeants, assets and inactive, as well as pensioners, if they manifested supporting the President of the Military Club, General of Brigade Helio Ibiapina Lima, that together with the Naval Club and of Aeronautics, they are struggling so that PEC, in walking in the Congress is modified of such a luck that excludes, definitively, the military ones, and the Mr. President can, in consequence, to accomplish his reiterated promises of guaranteeing them a system peculiar "previdenciário" and no linked to the National Institute of Social Sureness (WELFARE DEPARTMENT) (Colonel José Aldo Peixoto Corrêa).

Finally he asked: in face of the exposed the case of the military of the Reservation would not be and done Reform, meet together from Oiapoque to Chuí, in movement "reivindicatório" and moving to Brasília, in motorcade, just as they have been making other several classes with the objective of an end to put in so many threats, discriminations and humiliations?

Such a movement would be to give one is enough to everything that wrong and unjust it is happening, with the armed forces, in our companions' of the active face they have not conditions of doing it.

As for the remuneration (the increase) we cannot guide ourselves for examples of you judges, cause, military they don't make strike. However a small surprise readiness in Federal District, would make a lot of water to roll " under the bridge ".

Without a doubt ABEMIFA he understood the meaning of our ALERT Editorial " Partners on alert!"

That the example thrives, among the dispersed associations for whole Brazil!

On 2nd and 5th of month the Military Club will try to gather the associations the one that referred the colonel José Aldo, presenting them the bases of a system of peculiar Precaution to the military and independent of Treasury.

* President of the Military Club.

Index

Shoulder to Shoulder. May 2000. Page2.

Qu'est-ce that reads Tiers État?

Kurt Pessek

The the five hundred year-old unlucky party - the people pay but he doesn't enter - he forced me to review the beginnings of the French Revolution, source of all our basic social concepts. On that time, did it echo strong Emmanuel-Joseph Seiyès's revolutionary pamphlet, done know by Abbé Seiyés–with the title " THE ONE what is the Third State?" He explained to the people the value of turning the third force of decision in France to oppose the King and the Clergy. Above the rules, of the laws voted, above the basic beginnings, he defended the illustration of the national " will: The national will..., he only needs his reality to be legal, it is the origin of all legality." In other words, the proven desire of most has, in any moment, legality above the Constitution.

Last more than two centuries, in spite of king and clergy they inexist to serve as scapegoats, the people are still the great indigent in our country. Our representative system reveals unacceptable distortions. The elect for the people never defended his/her voters' beginnings because established and worse commitment, the following day to the election inexists, he breaks up with the origin and raisin to do part of the curse known by head political class.

They demand to be distinguished by category, they join to defend their wages and rights, to fortify mutual protections. Some, amaze, they leave inheritance for children and grandchildren. It is evident the inclination of the spirit of the popular representation whose larger consequence is to allow to small group of politicians to crystallize in true First State, rude usurpation. The Second is constituted by the protected of the elect ones, they begin young to suck in the sinecures and they finish ministers of the countless and useless tribunals. Those also stop being people, they become privileged breed.

The false backrest of the whole system consists of the call democracy, whose essence lives in the popular vote. Now, more vicious than our electoral politics. The call " national " will, the larger reason of the legality divulged by the elect ones, it is translated by the periodic voting in system without supporting fidelity, without ties in districts, when the parties, with unshame, sell legends, when the purchase of the vote is mood without shame, when the smart fox deceives the fool crow to do him to loosen the succulent cheese–the vote. In less than twenty-four hours it happens the miracle. Any "banabóia", without study or competence, without same knowledge how to administer the simplest cellar, to the raisin to be chosen doctor to be called and he/she begins to give hunches on all subjects. "Rebusnam" philosophy, moral "ornejam", "asneiam" laws, "tolejam hermenêutica", "sandejam deontologia" and.... they fill the she-ass with the money of the treasury, besides guaranteeing the permanence in I arrange him the any price.

The uncommon size of the representative anomaly can, now, to be well delineated. The current government if he/she chose with speech left "popularesco. "It was enough to arrive to the Power to change the "milonga". He governs with temporary measures, he bought the reelection to the Congress, he sold our grandparents' inherited patrimony, it protects the banks while they increase the poverty and the violence... finally, the promised leftist paradise ended, truly, in the hell of the multinationals, in the catastrophe of the unemployment with hunger, in the vortex of the robbery to the clever ones, in the bitterness of the disillusion. The researches point the unrestricted rejection of the Brazilians to the Government but anything if he can do because the "anojadiço" Prince ploted with most of the Congress. And the call " national " will of Seiyés, the origin of all legality " ends in the gutter, in spite of in theory to be worth more than all of them together wrapped in our comical Constitution.

kconsult@bsb.nutecnet.com.br

Thanks to microsoft office update and his partners

Next

Page 73

The inhuman dissembling tyranny

Vice Admiral Sérgio Tasso Vásquez of Aquino.

The essence of the true democracy is the virtue and, in the case of the western countries, of having marked Christian influence, the government action should still be guided by the search of the accomplishment of the Very Common, in atmosphere of justice and peace, with total respect to the human being inalienable rights, done to the image and similarity of God.

The democratic rulers, and the representatives of the people, in the true democracy, are male and women honored, that they surrender to their occupations with mission spirit, so only dedicated to serve, to donate their talents in benefit of the fellow citizens elevation, to exercise, with total responsibility and with altruism and patriotism copies, the authority portions that they are invested.

The atmosphere social, economical and political, in the true democracy, is harmonious, all are respected and they obey the wise and even laws, based on the fear to God and in the love to the fellow creatures. The citizens surrender, together, to stimulant and meritorious task of assuring worthy life for all, to build a nation more and more fair and strengthened in the soul, to guarantee a future always more smiling for the descendants...In a true democracy, the permanent concern exists with the Rude " National Happiness, there considered much more important than any economical indicators!

In the true democracy, they are reverenced, they are worshipped, they are evoked, as authentic patrimonies common to all, the past, the history, the values and the traditions; she battles, with all the forces of the body and of the soul, to improve the present; they rush the bases, she builds the roads, are dreamed the projects of a radiant future...Compassion exists for the weak ones, for the humble ones, for those excluded, to the which opportunities of progress and ascension are given, inside of the mark of the charity and of the respect to the citizenship, in a to share conscious of talents and talents: who more it received more if it is stimulated to give!

We wanted a true democracy to Brazil. How many patriots, along the History, were sacrificed and they were immolated to accomplish that ideal! As we are far, however, of rendering it!

So many fill the mouth to speak of democracy among us, wanting to do to believe that that is our regime! They are usually the imprudent, naive, or the ones that if fill their pockets mercilessly of the caricature that collected , and that she is perpetuating in the power like this unjust and distorted like this! Democracy as, if sizes are the poverty, the injustice, the exploration of the weakest and poor, the contempt for the people's rights, the indifference before the violence numberless, the irresponsible alienation of the national wealth, inheritance of the past, warranty of the present and safe for the future, for external centers of being able to, what does no commitment have with Brazil and the well-being of his people, the delivery of the sovereignty and of the national administration of the destinies of the Homeland?

The tyranny is installed among us with assumed apparels of democratic formalism; yes, only the form, any content! What was already bad worsened a lot of 1990 for here, with the coming of the imposition neoliberal leads to globalism, that assumed forums of terrifying asphyxia since 1995. An arrangement political "the best" is guaranteeing the approval of all the measures of the shift government's interest for the Congress, in that the parties vote for in block, as organized supporter, without entering in the merit of the cash it interests national, nor of ethical and moral reasons, but being subordinated, he/she saw of rule, to considerations of personal nature, grupal, corporate...The selfishness and the ambition for pieces of power, of participating in the benefits festival and privileges that it has been the prize of the ones that forget about the duties and contracted obligations with the credulous electorate, for only to think in advantages for the little " I ", they have been the lamentable tonic of the political practice. The rock down of temporary measures, that they are republished continually, more it accentuates the dictatorial character of the political administration and, when the will that order, of the president that she have faith anointed by the grace and almighty, one see impeded of prospering, due to constitutional obstacle, he moves the Constitution with the support of the helpful, obedient and loose parliamentary majority...High it has been the price pay, from the monstrous payment of the " it is giving that it is received ", until the deep sad and serious results political, economical, social and moral current of the government action in course.

The lie, the intense deceiving "propaganda" and to it weigh of gold transmitted, the version virtual triumphant official word of government that it is put upon to the hard and sad reality; the spread of the corruption, of the violence and of the impunity; the exacerbation of the injustice and of the poverty; the way to poverty of the middle class and the persecution to the public servants, to the retired ones; the salary earners fiscal exploration and the subsidies and the exemptions granted to the privileged ones, banks and national companies and foreigners; the donation of the national patrimony to the foreigner; the submission to centers of decisions of power, that it is configuring picture of growing spoilt limitation to the sovereignty begin to be noticed sharply, for the people, as perverse result of the dissembling tyranny in " democracy ' ' that makes unhapiness comes Brazil. They increase, for the whole part, the lack of comfort manifestations with the tragic direction of the events, as more and more perceptible they are the symptoms of disaggregation of the social fabric, as generalization and "banalização" of the violence, without the attendance of effective and efficient official measures to give him collect; spread of the drug traffic; It

45

dismiss desperate and in continuous ascension; "sucateamento" (to let it die for otself) of the systems of health and sanitation, precaution, education, house; deviations of indispensable public resources for private bills, in the succession of scandals that they wait " for sine-die " for the long, however late arm of the law...

It is done well-known - with all of the risks and involved dangers - the divorce among the government, the current apparatus of power, and the Nation, for fault of the first, that it returned the backs to the people and the legitimate interests of Brazil, configured in the search of the Development with Safety, in the Permanent National Objectives, forgetting - if that the ruler's first mission is the one of serving, being devoted, with the whole soul, to promote it Very Common with total respect to the larger values of the nationality, consolidated in his already long and suffered, but brave, noble and glorious History.

We trusted God All Powerful and in the dedication and in the competence of the Brazilians worthy of that name, however, to redeem and to rescue ours so loved Country, moving away the frightening spectra of the great convulsions of 1789, in king Luiz XVI'S France, and of 1917, in Russia of the czar Nicolau, that you patrol the horizons, and allowing the enthronement of the true democracy among us, for democratic authentic patriots, followers to Brazil, full of fear to the Mister God and with love in the heart for the people of our Earth!

That we can, for the force of the High and the effort of our talent, to see the Fifth Centennial of our Homeland already appear with radiant splendor, for the certainty of the liberation of the inhuman dissembling tyranny! That Brazil is the Earth of the Hope again, of the promise of the fraternal love, of the justice, of the peace!

Go Back

Page74

Shoulder to Shoulder, June 2000.

Editorial

Moment of decision

The edition previous of this newspaper was in the press when the press began to deflagrate one more ostensible attack campaign and disrepute of the Brazilian armed forces (F.A.B.), with the retaking of the molded accusations on the involvement of military Brazilian in the call Operação Condor. Now, we were already with the closed edition when the newspaper THE Globe brought to the dance the case of the confrontation of the river "had Betrayed", where, in 1991, an advanced position of the Army was attacked by guerrilla fighters of the Revolutionary armed forces of Colombia (FARC). According to the newspaper, based on the depositions of former-military and to of a " guerrilla commander ", the dead Colombians in the Brazilian retaliation would not have been guerrilla fighters, but simple prospectors. The two cases were followed to the attempt of reopening of the "Riocentro Affair", that occupied the news sections during some weeks and it was buried opportunely by Brazilian Superior Military Tribunal (STM.)

As mentioned already here in several opportunities, those events are not fortuitous nor they assist to a legitimate interest in the search of the truth. To the opposite, they answer to a bad covered strategy of maintaining the military ones Brazilian in permanent check and to impede them that show at this time critical. In the same context they interfere the trial balloons inflated amid the inquietude wave and popular indignation with the worsening of the urban and rural violence: the involvement of F.A.B. in the combat to the criminality, the extinction of the military police, the creation of a structure of federal control on the state police and even, amaze, the National Guard's re-birth (proposed openly rejected by the President, maybe, for remembering of the" Military Subject" of the end of the Empire). Concerning the suggestion of transforming the military ones in policemen, defended by senator Antonio Carlos Magalhães, we hoped she serves at least to demonstrate the true face of this grotesque illustration to their sympathizers among F.A.B.

All this happens amid the escalade of deterioration of the national life in all their aspects. In the economical field, the dilapidation of our public and private patrimony continues, with the insistence in the privatization of Banespa, the sale of actions of Petrobrás in hands of BNDES and the incessant denationalization than it still remains of the great Brazilian companies - just in the last days, the sales of the net of supermarkets were announced Bompreço, the largest of the Northeast, and of Villares, one of the largest industrial groups of the Country. This for not mentioning the let it dies of F.A.B., symbolized by the deterioration of the fleet of the Brazilian air force, that she has more than 60% of their aircrafts stopped by lack of replacement pieces and their reduced pilots to an insignificant number of hours of flight. The process is shown with more intensity in the field pshyco-social, in that the despair and the discouragement of the great majority of the vain Brazilians if transforming quickly in indignation and anger. Then it results a culture broth that makes way for facts a little suitable with the Brazilian nature, as physical aggressions to authorities or a more and more probable widespread social convulsion.

Before of that picture "dantesco", government authorities and their close followers they get ready in denouncing a " threat " to the institutions. Truly, the permanent institutions of the Nation were never so threatened, but for the harmful action of the Government more anti-national of the History of Brazil. Let us don't disguise: we spoke about a dictatorship civil democracy dressed, in the which, with the complicity of the political class and of the media, the Executive's boss governs for temporary measures and he suffocates financial and economically the Country, in benefit of the sacrosanct " investors' " interests, mainly the foreigners. In this context, he doesn't admire that, according to the press, His Excellency has traveled to Europe worried with the dissatisfaction symptoms among the military ones, as the ones that we mentioned in the previous editorial.

It is necessary that the Brazilians conscious, civil and military, join against the perspective of disintegration of the Country, front to which urges a firm position socket. To the that fear eventual external reactions, it is worth to remind the Brazilian performance in the meeting of Permanent Council of American Stataes (OEA), where, together with Mexico, our diplomacy led the Latin-American reaction to the pretension of the USA of considering illegitimate the recent presidential elections in Peru and to decree sanctions against this country. There it was clearly demonstrated that our Country has political density not only to head a reaction process against the misundertandings of the globalization , as, stiller, to impose their interests in the international scenery. Therefore, we cannot continue allowing that the opportunists' ambitions, the short-sightedness of the mediocre ones, the lack of courageous of the weak and the lunatic of the incendiaries take us inexorably to an unprecedented disaster in our history. This is the moment of decision. Tomorrow, it can be late too much.

Index

Page 75.

Shoulder to Shoulder. July 2000.

Editorial

The message of Ibirapuera

Suggestive and very opportune it was the ceremony accomplished by the Military Command of the Southeast, in São Paulo, SP, in the morning of 26 of last June, in honor to Sergeant Mário Kozel Filho, sacrificed, 32 years ago, for a coward action terrorist, when it accomplished his soldier duty, as sentry in the Headquarters of that Command. He lost the life as a consequence of the action of a car-bomb thrown against that Military Organization, headquarters of the referred homage in the Park of Ibirapuera.

It emphasizes to say that the reverence to Sergeant's Mário Kozel Filho memory, done annually, in any previous opportunity it had the magnificence of the event accomplished on this year. The homage, in the circumstances in that they happened, it takes us to a deep reflection.

First, because the extraordinary exaltation of patriotism and military honor that there it was demonstrated, it was an incentive to the soldier's soul that offers his/her life to the service of the Homeland, with direct reflexes in the invigoration of the morals of the troop, contaminating of enthusiasm and patriotism the high number of present civilians to the action. The armed forces don't offer "prebendas" nor any material goods; no put on the market, neither buy votes nor consciences. The only pays, for recognition to services, he/she translates himself in honor and dignity.

2nd, As, because it revealed a military leadership that it is not more willing to maintain arrested the armed forces to a pseudo fault compound that, "ardilosamente" try to impinge them, for inspiration of interests against our national ones, a lot of times moved from the foreigner, that they look for to relegate to the what it is not remembered the fundamental paper of the Army in the formation of the Brazilian nationality, from the most remote times and their permanent values. Remember here, that the current Governments of the Movement of 31 of Março of 1964, left of the national political scenery without compromising, without negotiating, without impositions of any nature but so only for own and unilateral decision, when they judged accomplished his/her mission. Opportune, also, it is to stand out that in spite of insidious propaganda adverse, same the new generations of the Army keep alive in the memory the words of the then Minister of the Army, General Walter Pires, that, on behalf of the Institution, he said: "We will always be solidary with those that, in the hour of the aggression and of the adversity, they accomplished the hard to owe of fighting back agitators and terrorists, of weapons in the hand, so that the Nation was not taken to the anarchy ".

Third, showed evident signs that the armed forces, in the opportune moment, they can leave aside their behavior of tolerance to retaliation attitudes taken to cable by many of the ones that formerly they drifted and they executed terrorist actions and today they occupy important public functions or they are invested generously of parliamentary immunities thanks to the amnesty granted by the Government, to which so much hate devotes; an unrestricted hate for the closet shame of the defeat that they suffered in the field of the weapons.

Finally, the solid presence of important leaderships of the civil world, in that solemnity, translates the testimony of the Brazilian society and his/her hope in the disposition of the Army in doing to prevail the supreme values of the Nation, in the instant in that in the sky of the Homeland black clouds that presage moments of turbulence in the political and social life of the Country appear.

That the homage to Sergeant Mário Kozel Filho serves as an alert to the enemies of the armed forces, that insist on reducing them the value and the presence in the national scenery.

Index

Page 76

Shoulder to Shoulder

http://www.ombro.com.br

August, 2000.

Editorial

Globalization = corruption

Malcolm - Which was the most recent misfortune?

Ross - That of one hour behind is already so old that they scoff who announces her. Every minute a new one is generated.

(Shakespeare, Macbeth, Action 4, Scene 3)

If we change the word " misfortune " for " scandal ", William Shakespeare's characters' lament is adjusted Brazil perfectly today, where the Federal Government's credibility, the respect to the political institutions and the trust in a true democracy space it is consuming every day, drowned by a tide amount of corruption and contempt by the citizenship, whose end doesn't seem to be to the view. In this picture, of little it will advance the explicit euphoria of the palatial circles and of the media engaged before the presidential former-secretary's Eduardo Jorge assumption " good acting " in the undercomission of the Senate. The case is far away from contained and, difficultly, it imitates it of slapstick set up for the deposition will impede that most explained of the population it stays with the discouraging impression that, as it was sketched in first Fernando's (Fernando Collor de Melo) space of time on presidency, the current Government (Fernando Henrique Cardoso) doesn't pass of an efficient platform for crooked deals of every type.

On the other hand, the verification that decanted " the globalization " has an element intrinsic that causes corruption doesn't limit to our Country. In many other, the perception is enlarged that the " theory of globalization " and the "modernity " that it is attributed her constitute excuses for a colossal process of transfer of public patrimony for "investors' select groups", denationalization and concentration of the control of the productive activities and of income, in a scale unprecedented reports. The example "paradigmatic" (pattern) is Mexico, where Carlos Salinas de Gortari Government (1988-94) it lotted the national economical infrastructure among a small group of his assistants, it increased from three to 26 the number of billionaires (in dollars) Mexican and it accentuated the economical breaking down that it culminated with the crisis of December of 1994. No by chance, Salinas of Gortari, who came from the University of Harvard and intimate of the high international finance - that intended to do the president of the World Organization of Trade of him - it finished his mandate dived in accusations of high corruption, that were worth a brother a prison sentence and to him own a himself-exile of several years.

The governments' legitimacy is obtained less by the number of votes that they receive in the elections, but, much more, for the dedication to the beginnings of the justice and of the very common, to the idea of the public thing, to the notion that the progress and the well-being of the citizenship should occupy the center of the formulation of the public politics. Such precepts emerged together with the institution of the sovereign national State, for the that is not coincidence to be one of the main objectives of the offensive " done by globalization followers ". The " global theory " provides the motto for the transformation of the public thing in a " cosa nostra " of the groups that control and they involve the established powers - as, unfortunately, we witnessed in Brazil. The result is a society in disaggregation, constituted of a contradictory mass of individuals without a sense of collective interest, merely concerned in satisfying personal ambitions or, in the other end, dominated by the survival difficulties amid the destruction of citizenship. In other words, a society in the which intends to do Bernard Mandeville's ideal to prevail, in that the sum of the individual perversions would be redundant in the public welfare - actually, closer of the fight of all against all suggested by Thomas Hobbes.

Only a wise exit exists for that problem of citizenship, that is a new invigoration of the sovereign national State, with the consequent re-establishment of public politics based on the republican beginning of the promotion of the justice and of the very common. In Brazil, as this it implicates in contradicting powerful established interests, national and transnational, difficultly the reconstruction of the national State can release the contest of an on purpose and vigorous civic-military alliance. Consequently, the future of our Country will depend on the urgency with that she settles down and consolidate.

next

Page 77

Shoulder to Shoulder. September 2000.

http://www.ombro.com.br

Editorial

Operation Itororó

In recent declarations on the aggravation of the violence in the Country, the Minister-boss of Institutional Safety's Cabinet, General Alberto Cardoso, it has been emphasizing that the situation is arriving the a " no-return " point. To face the problem, it proposes the accomplishment of a " national " crusade.

The violence is a phenomenon with many faces, for which these pages are limited even for a superficial discussion. However, it jumps to the eyes that its worsening accompanies to growing deterioration of the national life in all of the aspects - institutional, ethical, economical, social etc. - whose consequences converge in the loss of perspective of a worthy future for the great majority of the population, factor that the historians appear as relentless cause of overthrown civilization.

In response to General Cardoso's appeal, the Group Guararapes emitted a vigorous manifesto summoning " a national crusade to defend the Homeland and not to cover those that stab her". The manifesto suggests although one of the probable causes of that dramatic situation is the jettison of the armed forces of the process decision of the national politics.

Group Guararapes's manifestations represent a small expression of the intense fermentation that is verified in the breast of the Brazilian society, perceptible in the whole Country, giving opportunities the spontaneous formation of citizens' groups - uniformed and civilians - that look for an exit for the very national crisis. As we have been reiterating here, it is undelayable a firm socket of position of the conscious citizenship in face of the perspective of disintegration of the Country, today, maybe, more serious than confronted it by the Patron of the Army, Luís Alves de Lima e Silva, in the several victorious campaigns in that it guaranteed the national unit combining the highest soldier qualities and statesman.

The spirit of Caxias was reminded by the leader of the Army, General Gleuber Vieira, in the Order of the Day of August 25, when he asked that " all the members of the Army, uniformed or no, of the active or of the reservation, shoulder to shoulder, join around the same ideals for him protected. The challenges of the lived times will be overcome with the practice of the virtues demonstrated by Duque de Caxias and when each one of you, soldiers, to mobilize the loaded will in the energy of the words that his Patron pronounced in Itororó: 'Follow me the ones that are Brazilians!' "

One day before, when receiving the Medal Pedro Ernesto of the City hall of Rio de Janeiro, the military commander of the East, General Luiz Gonzaga Schroeder Lessa, it reaffirmed the paper of " an efficient one moderator power " that has been carried out by the military ones in the Brazilian history. At the same time, he emphasized that we were proud " of being an active agent in cementing of the feeling of nationalism that allows, thanks to God, to maintain united this multiracial and unharmed people the immense territorial base that we received from our ancestors and that so much became conceited ". Continuing, he said the General Lessa: We are " obedient and followers to the rigid discipline of the barracks, but never obsequious... We are silent, but never omitted and indifferent to the that happens in the four corners of the Homeland. We cultivated the patience as virtue, but we are never insensitive to the suffering of our people. We are simple for our own nature, but intellectual able and politically to read and to understand the national moment."

In his speech, the General Lessa observed that the fact little common of a professional soldier to be honored by a Legislative House reflects the established " bows in benefit of causes common to the people to who we served ". The danger of the Brazilian situation requests that the union among civilians and military it is deepened with the immediate formation of patriotic nuclei that they are ready for the defense of the Nation, whose decisive moment comes before us.

Page78

http://www.ombro.com.br

National crusade

Group Guararapes

All that are going to receive and to read this document will be conscious of how dangerous the moment in that we lived.

Those that attend the depressing picture of the depositions accomplished in Undercomission of Justice of the Senate or in some CPI they are to ask the presents are people of this world. All interrogate and asked them answer with details. At the end, nobody knows about anything and nor he/she heard to speak of 169 million of real (1 USD = 1,77 Real). They sign the documents and they are not responsible, because they received orders and who gave them, also, they are ignored by them. Two conclusions can be reached of everything this: the system of bureaucratic control of the public budgets or it is not accomplished or it is the most perfect of the world. The budget leaves the treasure. The work is not finished. The money disappears. The whole paper work demonstrates that everything is legal. The responsible suffer of lack of memory, they don't know anybody and they are of a cynicism that irritates the noblemen senators. Senator Heloisa Helena, from Alagoas, almost loses the such calm her intimate revolt, because she felt that she was making ridiculous paper in the highest House of the Legislative Power. It passed for the history the physiognomy of the senator's Pedro Simon fright, when in CPI of the Banks, one of those interrogated affirmed that whether he didn't remember 6 million Real that had been him given and put by him in his declaration of the income tax. It is too much. EVERYTHING CONTINUES IN THE BEST OF THE WORLDS.

The Dear Mr. President, that was 12 years senator and he is 6 years old already almost in President's position and that he saw uncoiling of the dwarfs' CPI, he affirms, only now, that there is no control in the public accounts in Brazil. The serious is that no objective measure was directed by His Excellency for defense of the treasury. The interesting is that when assuming the government put an end to the Special Commission of Investigation (CPI) and he put an end to the documents that the great rabbles that assaulted the public safes appeared. Does it give to understand?

They astonish us the declarations done by the Exmo. Mr. General Alberto Cardoso, in Rio de Janeiro, and published by the Leaf of São Paulo, of August 18. He affirmed the Mister general, when it analyzed the serious problem of the violence, the following: we are arriving close of a point of it doesn't return ". It is almost the recognition of the total bankruptcy of the State. The incredible is that the armed forces, that " they are destined to the defense of the Homeland, to the warranty of the constitutional powers and, for initiative of any of these, of the law and of the order " they were not consulted and, maybe, for this reason it is that we arrived to the current state. Senator Geraldo Melo, in recent speech, analyzed with a lot of clarity the importance of the armed forces in this context. The General Cardoso says although " the exit to control the violence is the accomplishment of a NATIONAL CRUSADE."

The GRUPO GUARARAPES is preaching, 9 years ago, this NATIONAL CRUSADE. The larger violence is not the abrupt death in the street. The violence is the ethics lack and of morals of those that should give the example. It is stolen, it is assaulted, it is lied, it is swindled, it is corrupted and he defends criminals and the Powers of the Republic deteriorate.

Terrible it is that they are buying consciences. We will make a NATIONAL CRUSADE to defend the Homeland and not to cover those that stab her. Be his part. Brazil depends on you! Publish this document!

We are Alive! August/2000

index

Page 79

http://www.ombro.com.br

Editorial

Electoral Transformism

The recent municipal elections provided to the attentive observers of the scenery national two quite evident data. The first was a great manifestation of the protest vote against the Federal Government and his neoliberal politics of alienation of the larger interests and of the patrimony of the Nation to the appetites of a privileged small group. In this matter, the merit is very larger of His Excellency and his suite than of Party of the Workers (PT) and of the other opposition parties. The second verification is that the government cupola was full aware of the proportions in that such vote would show and it moved the lines that it was able to strengthen PT, at the same time in that weakened less obsequious and more critical allies, as it happened with the mayor Roberto Magalhães, in Recife (Pernambuco).

In São Paulo (SP), after it defeats of his candidate in the first shift, the president Fernando Henrique Cardoso and his close apparatus everything did to promote candidate of PT, old visitor of the same circles that the Supreme Agent, his wife and close friends as the former-minister José Gregori, the minister José Serra, secretary Aloysio Nunes Ferreira and other. Already thinking about the elections of 2002, the government cupola thinks that a " PT of FHC " can be a possible alternative for the maintenance of the project " globalista ", given the previsible difficulties that the current official coalition can introduce a candidate viableto win elections and, no minus, the fact that the leaderships of PT have been demonstrating a convenient conformism before the dictates of the call " globalização ".
The political invigoration of PT presents an additional advantage for the President project of continuing with the breaking down of the national security apparel, that, as we already affirmed in this page, it is the counterpoint - practiced together with the left - of the breaking down of the economical structures of the Brazilian State - executed with the political right and with a small group of old leftists converted to the delicacies of the primacy of the markets ".

Without any allusion to the personal inclinations of the new stars of the constellation petista, as to mayor elected of São Paulo, all this represents the most evident and deplorable electoral transformism, that it justifies the crescents questions on the type of " effective democracy " in this suffered Country.

index

Agenda, diary, calendar. Nehemias Carneiro

Agenda

Rudyard Kipling: "Se podes manter o bom senso e a calma, num mundo a delirar, para quem o louco és tu,"

"If you can maintain the commom sense and the calm, in a world to be delirious, for who the lunatic is you,"

24.12.92 - Maria Luísa Fernandes Oliveira.

Colégio Compacto. Asa Norte. Mecânica Irmãos Gravias.

Em frente ao Banco Central. Ia pegar ônibus para Sobradinho.

Janeiro de 1993.

03 - Clínica de Repouso Planalto. 61-389-2012.

Conjunto Residencial Casa 3, CR-30, Vale do Amanhecer. Planaltina. 61-389-4776.

11 - Fuga da Clínica Planalto.

Rede Globo, Secretaria de Justiça, policial militar, bombeiro, QG do Exército, Cel., Maj. Brum - DProm, GAC, BGP, BPEB - Ten. Ortiz

Pulei o muro à esquerda da entrada. Atravessei a pista até um morro que é preservado pelo Governo do Distrito Federal. Voltei à pista, peguei carona de um caminhão, andei, pedi para ir sem pagar num ônibus, desci perto das instalações da TV Globo.

Passei pelo Colégio Militar de Brasília, Secretaria de Justiça do DF - protocolo, passei por um Cel. Art. DGS, Maj. Brum - D Prom, até o Quartel-General do Exército. Fui ao Hotel de Trânsito duas vezes, na 2ª o Cel. encarregado reclamou para mim.

12 - Dra. Cássia.

1 haldol, 1 fenergan,

1 haldol, 1 fenergan, 1 comprimido vermelho.

Fui à Ajure-DF. Depois que saí do Banco, o Vanderli veio dizer-me que o Chefe estava chamando.

Lá voltando, o médico do Banco deu-me remédio, colocou-me numa ambulância que me conduziu à Clínica de Repouso Planalto.

I64824, TC.12.16.C6, brbm.

Marlice, Elisandro.

pf13 - help, pf14 - troca password, pf15 - logoff

pf16 - combr, pf17 - renpac, pf18 - vazio

pf19 - netmaster, pf20 - brcicp4, pf22 - vazio

pf23 - rose, pf24 - diversos

14 - Dra. Cássia. Genilce, Isabel, Dr. André tirar o amplictil.

15 - Funcionário BB trazido pelo Abel. Falar com Dr. Paulo - psicólogo, para me levar para casa.

16 - Internos Miguel Carlos Cruz e Silva, Fabiano Domiciano Gonçalves, Garagem Amazonas. Sion. Montes Claros. 38-221-6737.

Dr. Masahito Yoshinoi.

20 - Dr. Antilhon. Dr. Carlos Henrique.

Anankê. SHIS QI-21, Conj. 14, Casa 15 - Lago Sul.

16 h de 22.01.93.

Dr. Antilhon levou-nos, em seu carro, da Ajure ao Ceasp. Antes telefonou ao Dr. Carlos Henrique solicitando minha alta.

Dr. Carlos Henrique disse que iria sair de férias e renovou minha licença até 19.02.93.

21 - Haldol - 2 à noite

Carbolitium 300 mg: 1 de manhã, 1 de noite

Ir à Clínica Planalto.

Ir ao Ceasp-Bsb.

Comprar carbolitium 300 mg.

22 - Clínica Anankê. SHIS, QI-21, Conj. 14, Casa 15, Lago Sul. 366-1567

Ônibus 623, W3N

245-2644

Alugado apartamento por 19 dias.

Sônia Maria Felício.

Clínica Chagas Freitas.

Bloco 715, SCRN 714/715, Apto. Bloco E, Entrada 11.
273-5742

Fomos ao Ceasp. De lá o Abel conduziu-nos à Anankê.

23 - 274 - 7181 text="#000000" link="#0000EE" vlink="#551A8B"> Calendar

dd/mm/yy

Rudyard Kipling: "If you can maintain the common sense and the calm, in a world to be delirious, for who the lunatic is you, "

24.12.92 - Maria Luísa Fernandes Oliveira.

Compact school. North wing. Mechanics Irmãos Gravias.

In front of the Central Bank. She will catch bus to Sobradinho.

January of 1993.

03.01.93 - clinic of Repouso Planalto. 61-389-2012.

Group Residential House 3, CR-30, the Dawn Valley. Planaltina. 61-389-4776.

11.01.93 - escape from the Planalto Clinic.

Net Globe, General office of Justice, military policeman, fireman, Head Quarters of the Army, Col., Maj. Brum - DProm, GAC, BGP, BPEB - Lieutenant Ortiz

I jumped the wall to the left of the entrance. I crossed the track until a hill that is preserved by the Government of Federal district. I returned to the track, I hitchhiked of a truck, I walked, I asked to go without paying in a bus, I went down close to TV Globe's facilities.

I went by the Military School of Brasília, General office of Justice of DF - I record, I went by a Col. Artillery General Services Department, Maj. Brum - Promotion Department, until the Headquarters of the Army. I went to the Hotel of Traffic twice, in the 2nd Col. person in charge complained for me.

12.01.93 - Dra. Cassia.

1 haldol, 1 fenergan,

1 haldol, 1 fenergan, 1 red tablet.

I went to Ajure-DF. After I left the Bank, Vanderli came to tell me that the Boss was calling.

There returning, the doctor of the Bank gave me medicine, it put me in an ambulance that led me to Repouso Plateau's Clinic.

I64824, TC.12.16.C6, brbm.

Marlice, Elisandro.

pf13 - help, pf14 - it changes password, pf15 - logoff

pf16 - combr, pf17 - renpac, pf18 - empty

pf19 - netmaster, pf20 - brcicp4, pf22 - empty
pf23 - rose, pf24 - several

14.01.93 - Dra. Cassia. Genilce, Isabel, Dr. André to remove the amplictil.

15.01.93 - employee BB brought by Abel. To speak with Dr. Paulo - psychologist, to take me home.

16.01.93 - internal Miguel Carlos Cruz and Silva, Fabiano Domiciano Gonçalves, Garagem Amazonas. Zion. Montes Claros. 38-221-6737.

Dr. Masahito Yoshinoi.

20.01.93 - Dr. Antilhon. Dr. Carlos Henrique.

Anankê. SHIS QI-21, Conj. 14, house 15 - South Lake.

16 h of 22.01.93.

Dr. Antilhon took us, in his car, from Ajure to Ceasp. Before he called Dr. Carlos Henrique requesting my discharge.

Dr. Carlos Henrique said that would leave vacations and it renewed my license up to 19.02.93.

21.01.93 - Haldol - 2 at night

Carbolitium 300 mg: 1 in the morning, 1 at night

To go to the Planalto Clinic.

To go to Ceasp-Brasília.

To buy carbolitium 300 mg.

22.01.93 - clinic Anankê. SHIS, QI-21, Conj. 14, house 15, South Lake. 366-1567

Bus 623, W3N

245-2644

Rented apartment by 19 days.

Sônia Maria Felício.

Clinic Chagas Freitas.

Block 715, SCRN 714/715, Apartment. Block "E", Entrance 11.

273-5742

We went to Ceasp. From there Abel led us to Anankê, in a Bank car.

23 - 274 - 7181

22.01.93 - Clínica Anankê. SHIS, QI-21, Conj. 14, Casa 15, Lago Sul. 366-1567 Ônibus 623, W3N

245-2644

Alugado apartamento por 19 dias.

Sônia Maria Felício.

Clínica Chagas Freitas.

Bloco 715, SCRN 714/715, Apto. Bloco E, Entrada 11.

273-5742

Fomos ao Ceasp. De lá o Abel conduziu-nos à Anankê.

23.01.93 - 274 - 7181

24.01.93 - 1ª aula de desenvolvimento na irmandade do Vale do Amanhecer - Tia Neiva.

25.01.93 - Dona Rita, dona da pensão no Vale do Amanhecer, ainda não apresentou a conta.

Telefonema da Joyce - Ceasp - Bsb.

Telefonema para Sônia - encarregada do aluguel do apartamento na W3N.

Reunião com Dra. Paula, psiquiatra, e Joana, psicóloga.

February, 1993.

08.02.93 - Fomos à Anankê dizer que estaríamos viajando para o Maranhão.

A Maria Helena, psicóloga, pediu-nos para apanharmos no Ceasp autorização para tratamento no mês de fevereiro.

09.02.93 - Comprei as passagens na BB-Tur.

P10.02.93 - Saída de manhã de táxi.

Francisca foi entregar chaves do apartamento no DESED.

15:00 Chegada em Caxias.

15.02.93 - Consulta com Dr. Mardônio em Teresina.

Receitou 90 dias de licença.

19.02.93 - Licença até 19.02.93. Este prazo foi alterado para 15 de maio de 1993.

March, 1993.

07.03.93 - José Neto prometeu devolver a bicicleta na Praça do Panteon, onde aguardava a Nely, que foi para reunião de crianças, convidada pela An, esposa do Nvd.

A bicicleta foi devolvida em 05.05.93.

08.03.93 - 10 pacotes de vela para dona Raimunda. Ten packs of candles to miss Raimunda.

27.03.93 - Vencimento do cheque-ouro de 5.000 na agência Central-Brasília.

April, 1993.

17.04.93 - An, mulher do Nvd, telefonou. Deixei recado na casa e comércio do Prr.

Seu Totonho, Mariinha, dona Raimunda, telefonaram.

19.04.93 - Falei com Nvd - sem novidades.

Prr - recebi extrato.

Tem 2 implantadores na agência.

22.04.93 - Nvd e Mdrs disseram que minha remoção chegou.

SBS - Bloco A - Plano Piloto.

70073-900

Telefone 212-2333 ações.

Uma explosão no carro do Nthn.

212-2311 Geafa/Davi.

24.04.93 - Fomos à casa de dona Raimunda. Rezamos um rosário e um terço.

22.01.93 - clinic Anankê. SHIS, QI-21, Conj. 14, house 15, South Lake. 366-1567

Bus 623, W3N

245-2644

Rented apartment by 19 days.

Sônia Maria Felício.

Clinic Chagas Freitas.

Block 715, SCRN 714/715, Capable. Block AND, Entrance 11.

273-5742

We went to Ceasp. From there Abel led us to Anankê.

23.01.93 - 274 - 7181

24.01.93 - 1st development class in the fraternity of the valley of the Dawn - Aunt Neiva.
25.01.93 - lady Rita, lady of the pension in it is Valley of the Dawn, it still didn't present the bill.

Phone call of Joyce - Ceasp - Bsb.

Phone call for Sônia - entrusted of the rent of the apartment in W3N.

Meeting with Dra. Paula, psychiatrist, and Joana, psychologist.

February, 1993.

08.02.93 - we went to Anankê to say that would be traveling to Maranhão.

Maria Helena, psychologist, asked us for us to take in the Ceasp authorization for treatment in the month of February.

09.02.93 - I bought the passages in BB-Tur.

10.02.93 - exit in the morning by taxi.

Francisca went to give keys of the apartment in DESED.

15:00 arrival in Caxias.

15.02.93 - it consults with Dr. Mardônio in Teresina.

He wrote prescriptions 90 days of license.
19.02.93 - license up to 19.02.93. This period was altered for May 15, 1993.

March, 1993.

07.03.93 - José Neto promised to return the bicycle in the Square of Panteon, where Nely, that went to children's meeting awaited, invited by An, it marries of Nvd.

The bicycle was returned in 05.05.93.

08.03.93 - 10 candle packages for lady Raimunda. Ten packs of candles to miss Raimunda.

27.03.93 - expiration of the check-gold of 5.000 in the agency Central-Brasília.

April, 1993.

17.04.93 - An, woman of Nvd, called. I left message in the house and trade of Prr.

Mr. Totonho, Mariinha, lady Raimunda, called.

19.04.93 - I spoke to Nvd - without innovations.

Prr - I received extract.

There are 2 functionaries from Methods and organization Department in the agency.

22.04.93 - Nvd and Mdrs said that my removal arrived.

SBS - Block THE - Pilot Plan.

70073-900

Telephone 212-2333 stocks.

An explosion in the car of Nthn.

212-2311 Geafa/Davi.

24.04.93 - we went to lady's house Raimunda. We said a rosary and a third.

www.ingramcontent.com/pod-product-compliance
Lightning Source LLC
Chambersburg PA
CBHW061519250726
48657CB00005B/1966